WHO CRUCIFIED JESUS?

*Nam quis nescit primam esse historiae
legem, ne quid falsi dicere audeat?
deinde ne quid veri non audeat? ne
quae suspicio gratiae sit in scribendo?
ne quae simultatis? haec scilicet fun-
damenta nota sunt omnibus.*

CICERO, *De Oratore*, 11, 15, 62.

Are not these the fundamental laws of
writing history? The historian dare
not tell any falsehood; he must be
bold enough to tell the whole truth;
he must not be suspected of favoritism
or prejudice.

By the same author

WHO CRUCIFIED JESUS?

By SOLOMON ZEITLIN

BLOCH PUBLISHING COMPANY
New York

WHO CRUCIFIED JESUS?

Fifth Edition

COPYRIGHT © 1964 BY BLOCH PUBLISHING COMPANY

Library of Congress Card Number: 64:7855
ISBN 0-8197-0013-4

PRINTED IN THE UNITED STATES OF AMERICA

PREFACE

In the year 1941 and the early part of 1942, I published in the *Jewish Quarterly Review* a series of studies entitled "The Crucifixion of Jesus, Re-Examined."

Some Christian scholars suggested that I publish the result of my studies in book form for the laity. I followed their suggestion. Although based on my original studies, this book contains considerable new material in addition to a new presentation of the backgrounds of the times in all their aspects.

In giving the last two chapters on the trial of Peter and Paul, my purpose was not only to show that they were tried by a political Sanhedrin and put to death by the Romans, but to present additional and conclusive evidence that at the time of Jesus there were two Sanhedrins.

Since this book is intended for the general reader, I have tried to avoid as much as possible any intricate notes. I have given only the most necessary references to the sources. The reader who seeks a more detailed analysis of the problems involved in this book is referred to my studies in the *Jewish Quarterly Review*.

The literature on the Gospels as well as on the life of Jesus is quite extensive and can be found in any good encyclopedia. However, I thought it advisable to give a selective bibliography for this literature published in the last two decades. Many of the books dealing with this subject I have reviewed in the pages of the *Jewish Quarterly Review*. I refer the reader to those issues in which they originally appeared.

v

The reader may notice that in the bibliography dealing with the life of the Jews and the sects during the Second Commonwealth, I did not refer to any Jewish works. It is with chagrin that I note that there is no literature written by Jews to which the reader may be referred. It is indeed rather strange that we should not have any literature written by Jews on this most important period in Jewish history, a period when Judaism was cemented, and had the greatest influence not only on the Jewish people but on civilization as well. We do have many books on this period written by Christian scholars. However, they have given preference to one set of sources—The New Testament and Josephus—while they have ignored or misunderstood the *Tannaitic* literature.

There is a saying that to know the poet one must go to the country of his birth. To write a history of the Jews of the Second Commonwealth a full and profound knowledge of the *Tannaitic* literature is indispensable.

In examining the trial of Jesus, I made use of all the sources available, namely, the different readings of the *Tannaitic* literature as recorded by Rabbinovicz in his *Variae Lectiones*, and, also, all the different readings quoted in the vast rabbinic literature; for Josephus, Niese's edition *Flavii Josephi Opera*; for Philo's Works, Cohn's, *Philonis Alexandrini Opera*; on the study of the Gospels, all the variant readings recorded by C. Tischendorf, H. F. Von Soden's edition of the New Testament, likewise the *Codex Sinaiticus* produced in facsimile from photographs by Helen and Kirsopp Lake;

for *The Acts*, in addition to the above-mentioned works, the texts of *The Acts* by J. H. Ropes, edited by F. J. Foakes Jackson, and Kirsopp Lake *The Beginnings of Christianity*. For the Apostolic Fathers I utilized the edition of Kirsopp Lake (in the Loeb Classical Library). Bearing in mind the fact that this book is intended for the general reader, in quoting biblical passages I gave preference to the King James and to the American Revised Version, except in instances where obvious necessity required the use of other translations based on manuscript readings.

It is with great pleasure that I record my profound gratitude to my friend, Dr. Mortimer J. Cohen, for his constant assistance to me with suggestions and counsel. In a genuine spirit of friendship, he was always at my service in helping me plan the book. I am under special obligation to him for his kindness in reviewing the entire manuscript and in making necessary revisions.

I am very grateful to the staff of Dropsie College for placing at my disposal all the necessary books.

CONTENTS

INTRODUCTION TO THE FIFTH EDITION

Since it became the cornerstone of Christianity, the crucifixion of Jesus has been a monumental event in the history of mankind. The Crucifixion has both a theological and an historical aspect. According to Paul, "Christ our Passover is sacrificed for us." (I Cor. 5:7); "Christ died for our sins according to the Scriptures." (Rom. 3:24); "And he had given himself for us as an offering and sacrifice to God." (Eph. 5:2)

From its beginning, the Church stressed the Crucifixion as the cornerstone upon which Christianity was built, that God in his infinite mercy gave his only son as a ransom for the sins of mankind. In the Epistle of Diognetus (IX), the anonymous author writes, "He Himself (God) gave his son as ransom for us, the holy for the wicked, the innocent for the guilty, the just for the unjust, the incorruptible for the corruptible, the immortal for the mortal." Justin Martyr (c. 100-165 C.E.) says that Christ was the Paschal Lamb, "for the pascha (Paschal Lamb) was Christ who was afterwards sacrificed . . . and as the blood of the pascha saved those who were in Egypt, so also the blood of Christ will save those who believed." (Dialogue with Trypho, 111).

The crucifixion of Jesus also belongs in the realm of history. The question of why Jesus was put to death must confront the historian. What capital offense had Jesus committed to warrant crucifixion? In presenting a case, an historian as well as a jurist must pierce through all available documents without prejudice. He must examine the events carefully and impartially. He must take notice of contradictions and discrepancies in the documents of the case. The motive which led to the commission of the act must be diligently scrutinized and investigated. With regard to the motive involved in the death of Jesus, the Judaeans had no reason to put Jesus on the cross. Jesus had not committed a

capital sin against their religion. In proclaiming himself to be
the Messiah, he did not commit a religious offense. Many
followers of the Pharisees—the Apocalyptics—looked forward to the day when the Messiah would reveal himself and
free them of the Roman yoke. Jesus' saying that he would
destroy the Temple and rebuild it in three days did not
constitute a capital sin warranting death. Nor did Jesus blas-
pheme against Yahweh. Furthermore if, for the sake of
argument, one assumes that Jesus *had* committed a capital
offense against the Judaean religion, it is equally reasonable
to assume that the Judaean Bet Din would have put him to
death by stoning. The High Court had the power to exact
and enforce death in the punishment of capital crimes.
Josephus, in *War VI*, ii, 4, writes that when Titus appealed to
the Judaeans to surrender, he said, "And did we not permit
you to put to death any who passed it (beyond the barrier to
the Sanctuary) even were he a Roman? Evidently, the
Judaeans had ful power to inflict capital punishment on
anyone who transgressed the Judaean religion by committing a capital sin.

Jesus was crucified, and Pilate ordered that an inscription
in Hebrew, Greek, and Latin be placed on the cross. The
inscription read as follows: *Jesus Nazarenus, Rex Iudaeorum,*
"Jesus of Nazareth, King of the Jews." This inscription de-
finitively proves that Jesus was executed as a political offender who had been considered by many of his followers to be
King of the Jews. The Roman custom was to record the
reason for execution and to place it on the cross of crucifixion.

In this book, I endeavor to demonstrate unequivocally
that the Jews had no interest in putting Jesus to death, that
he was, in fact, executed as a political offender.

In the text of "Guidelines and Suggestions for Implement-
ing the Conciliar Declaration Nostra Aetate (In our time),"
the Council recalled that "what happened in his passion
cannot be blamed upon *all* (italics mine) the Jews then living,

without distinction, nor upon the Jews of today." In other words, *some* of the Jews of that time are to be blamed for the crucifixion of Jesus, for they sought to destroy him for his religious offenses. It should, however, be reemphasized that Paul, in his Epistles, never accuses the Jews for the Crucifixion.

Irenaeus (c. 120-200C.E.) writes,

> It is clear that the Lord suffered death in obedience to His Father, upon that day on which Adam died while he disobeyed God. Now he died the same day in which he did eat. For God said, "On that day on which you shall eat of it, you shall die by death." The Lord, therefore, recapitulating in Himself this day, underwent his suffering upon the day preceding the Sabbath, that is the sixth day of creation on which man was created, thus granting him a second creation by means of His Passion, which is that (creation) out of death.

Jesus was crucified to redeem mankind from the Original Sin. There is no discrepancy in the Gospels as to the day of the Crucifixion. It occurred on Friday—the same day of Adam's Original Sin. If Jesus went to death in obedience to His Father, out of infinite love and to redeem mankind from Original Sin, how, then, can even *some* Jews be held responsible for the Crucifixion?

The Church holds proselytizing as a tenet. This is based on the dictum of Jesus given to the disciples when he appeared to them after the Resurrection: "Go you, therefore, and teach all nations, baptizing them in the name of the Father, the Son, and the Holy Ghost." (Matt. 28:19) Judaism, on the other hand, does not preach proselytism. Jews neither seek to convert others nor wish to be converted themselves.

In the "Guidelines," the following is mentioned: "With the prophets and the same Apostle (Paul), the Church awaits that day known to God alone on which all peoples will address the Lord in a single voice and serve Him with one accord." (Soph. 3:9) The Apostle Paul always applies the appelation "Lord" to Jesus. This is one of the diametrical differences between the Christians and the Jews in the Parting of the Ways.

In the Guidelines, dialogues between Christians and Jews are strongly urged; this is certainly desideratum. The Jews and Christians live on one planet, are members of one human society, and have a common interest in the welfare of their country. There is a great need for discussion between Christians and Jews on moral and social issues besetting our civilization. Other problems which might be discussed by both groups are such issues as energy, unemployment, and sex. But not religion. On this the Jews and Christians remain divided. They are two different religions with differing ideologies. While it is true that Judaism is the mother of Christianity, after the Parting of the Ways the two became distinct theologies. However, originally, Christianity was essentially a sect of Judaism. Frank discussions on the essence that now separates the two could give offense to one another, and this certainly is neither healthy nor desirable. Such a situation may lead to a monologue rather than a dialogue. The Jews throughout their history have shied away from dialogues with the Christians. It is true that during the Middle Ages there were dialogues between Christians and Jews, but these were forced upon the Jews, who were compelled to defend their faith. The so-called dialogue between Justin Martyr and Trypho was in reality a monologue. Justin placed arguments against Christianity in Trypho's mouth so that the latter might refute them. It is comparable to the dialogues that appear in the writings of Plato and Shakespeare. Even in this "dialogue," Justin had Trypho say that he regretted his rejection of the advice of the sages not to engage in dialogues with the Christians. Dialogue between Jew and Christian on religion is contrary to the history of Judaism. The Jews follow the maxim of the prophet Michah: "Let all the people walk each one in the name of his God, but we will walk in the name of Adonai, our God for ever and ever." The words of the prophet are quite applicable to our own days.

A paragraph in the "Guidelines" reads:

> Lest the witness of Catholics to Jesus Christ give offense to Jews, they must take care to spread their Christian faith while maintaining the strictest respect for religious liberty in line with the teaching of the Second Vatican Council (Declaration "Dignitatis Humanae"). They will likewise strive to understand the difficulties which arise for the Jewish soul——rightly imbued with an extremely high, pure notion of the divine transcendence—when faced with the mystery of the incarnate Word (logos).

This paragraph is stylistically obscure, and it may indicate the old principle of proselytizing. Again, in the phrase "incarnate word, "there is a doctrine of Christian theology. Cf. John (1:1-14, *passim*) "In the beginning was the word ... and the word was God ... and the word was made flesh and dwelt among us."

The following paragraph reads:

> An effort will be made to acquire a better understanding of whatever in the Old Testament retains its own perpetual value, since that has not been cancelled by the later interpretation of the New Testament. Rather, the New Testament brings out the full meaning of the Old, while both Old and New illuminate and explain each other.

This was the bone of contention that led to the Parting of the Ways between the Pharisees and the leaders of the new faith. This paragraph also serves to illustrate that dialogues between Christians and Jews are unhealthy and should not be held.

In the "Guidelines" there is a paragraph condemning Anti-Semitism:

> We may simply restate here that the spiritual bonds
> and historical links binding the church to Judaism
> condemn (as opposed to the very spirit of Christian-
> ity) all forms of anti-Semitism and discrimination,
> which in any case the dignity of the human person
> alone would suffice to condemn.

This paragraph is praiseworthy, for in it the modern
Church condemns anti-Semitism. However, it is to be noted
that the theology of the Crucifixion, by which the Church
emphasized that the Jews killed Christ, brought immeasura-
ble suffering and death to innocent people. It was a cruel
libelous accusation against the very people who gave Jesus to
the world. The Christian world must atone for *its* guilt of
propagating that the Jews crucified Jesus.

Anti Semitism is a cancer gnawing at the vitals of civilization. Although the Jews are the first and real victims of the
disease, ultimately it will become a pestilence that will strike
Christians as well. The primary aim of the Nazis was to
destroy the Jews and Judaism, but ultimately, their goal was
to destroy Christianity as well. Alfred Rosenberg, the Apostle of Nazism, held the view that Christianity was a religion of
slaves. The Nazis maintained that neither Protestantism nor
Catholicism expressed the soul of the German people. Their
motto was, "We must create a German Christianity," the
intent being to exchange the cross for a swastika.

In this book, after examining critically all the historical
and legal sources pertaining to the trial and execution of
Jesus, I have arrived at the verdict that neither the Jews nor
their leaders were responsible for the death of Jesus. Jesus
was crucified by the Romans as a political offender.

SOLOMON ZEITLIN

Dropsie University
June 10, 1975

INTRODUCTION
TO THE FOURTH EDITION
THE CRUCIFIXION OF JESUS,
A LIBELOUS ACCUSATION AGAINST THE JEWS

For eighteen centuries the Jews have been accused of the crucifixion of Jesus. To this day they are still called Christ killers, deicides. This grave charge, fraught with sorrow and suffering to the Jewish people, is still preached by some ministers of the gospel and taught to the children in the schools. It is recognized as a dominating factor in spreading and perpetuating anti-Semitism.

This accusation, propagated from the beginning of the second century, has continued to our own day. In this book I have demonstrated that the Gospels and the Apostolic Fathers did not place the onus of the crucifixion upon the Jews. The accusation was brought forward by the early leaders of the Church to show that the Jews, who originally were chosen people of God, were no longer chosen after they had crucified Jesus— God had forsaken them. Those who accepted Jesus as the true Messiah became the chosen people, the true Israelites. They held that the destruction of Jerusalem and the burning of the Temple by the Romans were a punishment for their guilt in the death of Jesus. This accusation was brought first to show the truth of Christianity, second to show that Judaism was no longer the true religion. It was theologically important for the leaders of the early Church to place responsibility for the crucifixion upon the Jews. Christianity was a new religion and they had to struggle to support it and to win recruits.

Some modern historians do recognize that a distinction must be made between the theology in connection with the crucifixion and the historical facts. Recently certain Christian theologians have maintained that the Jews should acknowledge the actual historical fact that their forefathers, the spiritual leaders, were responsible for the crucifixion, and that the Jews could eliminate anti-Semitism if they would make that admission.

The sources are the four Gospels, Mark, Matthew, Luke, and John. The first three are called the Synoptic Gospels. They are more or less in agreement in their accounts of the ministry of Jesus. The Gospel according to John is called non-Synoptic, since it differs from the others and there are many discrepancies. Although Mark, Matthew, and Luke are generally in agreement, nevertheless different versions are recorded regarding events in connection with the arrest and trial.

In this book I show that the Gospels are not historical books. Their authors were not interested in presenting the cold facts. They presented their theological conception of Jesus and his ministry. To them the resurrection as well as the crucifixion was the cornerstone upon which the new religion of Christianity was founded.

An impartial historian in presenting the facts of the trial and crucifixion must take cognizance of the differences in the accounts in the Gospels. It is also his duty to examine all the available manuscripts of the Gospels. To demonstrate this I have shown that in Mark X:33 which has, "Behold we go up to Jerusalem and the Son of man shall be betrayed to the chief priests and the scribes. And they shall condemn him to death, and shall deliver him to the Gentiles." In some manuscripts the word "death" is omitted. Such an omission cannot be ascribed merely to a scribal error. The Church in the Middle Ages thought that the Jews were responsible for the crucifixion of Jesus; therefore it is certain that the copyists had a manuscript which went back to the period before the Gospels were actually put into writing and canonized. The author of Mark accused the chief priests and the scribes only of delivering Jesus to the Gentiles but not of his death. Again in Mark III: 6 the text has, "And the Pharisees went forth and straightway took counsel with the Herodians against him, how they might destroy him." In some ancient Greek manuscript the text has "to deliver him" in place of "destroy him."

Jesus was arrested and put to death as a rebel against Rome, and was crucified as king of the Jews. On the cross was inscribed in Hebrew, Greek, and Latin: *Iesus Nazarenus, Rex Iudaeorum,* "Jesus of Nazareth, King of the Jews." It was the Roman custom to offer the reason for the execution, Pilate followed the established method.

This book was written from the historical angle, not the theological. I have demonstrated that the Jews are guiltless and cannot be blamed for the crucifixion. The Christian world must *atone* for their guilt towards the Jewish people for using the incident as a pretext for enslaving and persecuting the Jews throughout the ages. The accusation of being deicides accelerates anti-Semitism. The Jews need not apologize to the Christians; responsibility for the crucifixion cannot be put upon them for the acts of their forefathers. The verdict of this book is that the spiritual leaders of the Jews of that time were not guilty.

Judaism and Christianity are separate religions, each with its own theology. Though Christianity arose in Judaea and its founders were Jews, Christianity in the process of time became a Gentile religion. The founders of Christianity, to prove that Jesus was the true messiah Christ, based their assumptions on the Pentateuch and Prophets. Christianity arose as a Judaeo-Christian religion. The Jews of the Diaspora paved the way for the Apostles to the Gentiles to preach Christianity to the pagans. For centuries the Jews of the Diaspora preached and taught that there is only one God, that He is the God of the universe, that all men are equal before God regardless of race, that He is the God of all mankind.

The Jews do not wish to convert the Christians to Judaism nor to be converted to Christianity. Zalman Shazar, President of Israel, when he met Pope Paul VI in Israel, proudly emphasized the eternal words of the Prophet Micah:

Let all the peoples walk each one in the name of his god, but we will walk in the name of Adonai, our God forever and ever.

The great humanitarian and saintly Pope John XXIII, in the dark days of Jewish history when millions of Jews were destroyed and burned in the gas chambers for no crime but that they were Jews, interceded whenever he could and saved the lives of many. On Good Friday the Catholics, in praying for all peoples, have a prayer *pro perfidis Judaeis* and they ask God to have mercy on *Judaica perfidia.* Pope John ordered the words *perfidis* and *perfidia* be omitted. The present Pope Paul VI is following the steps of his great predecessor in summoning the Ecumenical Council.

We trust that this Council will show good will to the mother religion by removing the unjustifiable stigma from the Jews in declaring in its schema that historically the Jews are not guilty of the crucifixion of Jesus. This would erase the *guilt* of the Church for defamation of an innocent people, the people of the prophets.

SOLOMON ZEITLIN

July, 1964
Dropsie College

INTRODUCTION
TO THE THIRD EDITION

THIS book was written at the time of the holocaust when the free world was struggling for its existence; when six million Jews, almost a third of the people, were exterminated; when Jews were compelled to wear a yellow badge, the star of David, as they were led to the crematories. The Jews were destroyed for no crime against the state, only because they were Jews. It is true the Nazis did not annihilate the Jews because they crucified Jesus, but rather because they gave Jesus to the world. The Nazis knew that they had to destroy Judaism before they could abolish Christianity. We must bear in mind, however, that the Christian masses had been taught for many centuries that the Jews crucified Jesus, that they were deicides, and hence they came to look upon the Jews not as children of God, but as children of the devil. This is one of the reasons why the German people as well as other peoples fell victims to the demagogues and even helped them to destroy the Jews.

Judaphobia, otherwise known as anti-Semitism, began in the Diaspora; it was not, however, the Diaspora which led to ill-will toward the Jews; it was rather their idea that God was universal and the only God, and their doctrine that the deities of other nations were abominable idols not to be worshiped. The Jews refused to worship the god of the state or bow to him. They refused to participate in the libations in honor of the king. We repeat, it was their conception of the universality of God, in fact their intolerance of polytheism, that aroused hostility against them, not the Diaspora. At the time when the Jews had their own state, Judaea, thousands upon thousands were killed in many cities through the Hellenistic world. They were regarded as atheists who did not believe in a national god. Yet the fundamental Jewish belief in one God, and the uncompromising attitude towards national gods, paved the way for Paul, the apostle to the Gentiles, to preach his gospel and gain recruits from the pagan world. Thus the Jews of the Diaspora whose blood had been shed for upholding the idea of a universal God were in a great measure indirectly responsible for the spread of Christianity. Therefore, we may truly say that the blood of the Jewish martyrs in the Diaspora was the seed of the Christian Church.

The relationship of the Jews to the early Christians was not that of membership in a new religion. Christianity in the first century had not yet been crystallized into a religion separate from Judaism. The early Christians consisted mostly of Jews. The Jews looked upon them as *minim*, that is, heretics. There was animosity between these two groups; however, when Christianity became an independent religion separate from Judaism and its adherents consisted mostly of gentiles, the Jewish attitude towards Christianity changed. The Christians were no longer considered heretics or heathens. It was recognized that the Christians believed in the universality of God and were not idol worshipers.

The Church Fathers, beginning with the second century, brought the charge against the Jews of crucifying

Jesus. Justin Martyr was the first to do so. This charge was brought to the fore by the subsequent Church Fathers. The Apostolic Fathers, however, never attributed the crucifixion of Jesus to the Jews. The Church Fathers maintained that God had forsaken the Jews because of their rejection and crucifixion of Jesus. This was the reason they assigned for the burning of the Temple, the destruction of the Jewish State, and their dispersion among the nations. The charge of the Church Fathers that the Jews were deicides, the killers of Jesus, has been a battle cry since the second century. The charge that the blood of Jesus was perpetually upon the hands of the Jews was stressed through the Middle Ages. Many leaders of the Church at that time tried to protect the Jews from persecutions and pogroms. The masses could not understand why they were not permitted to kill the Jews since they had been taught that the Jews killed their Lord—deicides.

I made it clear in this volume that the Jews did not crucify Jesus, and that Jesus was tried by a state synedrion and not by a religious Sanhedrin. I wrote in this book, "As modern Quislings, puppet governments and puppet rulers, betrayed their peoples and become instruments to work the will of the conqueror, so in a world now passed away Jewish Quislings proved traitors to their own people that they might, for personal aggrandizement and power, to the bidding of Roman masters."

The theological as well as the lay reviewers, with few exceptions, were very sympathetic to the theories advanced in this volume. *The Christian Advocate,* the official organ of the Methodist Church, besides having a review of the book, carried an editorial in the January 22, 1948 issue entitled, "Who Crucified Jesus"? Because of the importance I assign to this editorial I reproduce it in toto with the kind permission of the former editor, Roy L. Smith, and the present editor, T. Otto Nall:

WHO CRUCIFIED JESUS?

"The Jewish people did not crucify Jesus.

"The Synoptic Gospels, Peter and Paul, and the Apostolic Fathers—in a word, the founders of Christianity, and the creators of the church—have never accused the Jewish people of the death of Jesus of Nazareth.

"The crucifixion of Jesus was committed by Pilate, the Roman procurator, not by the Jews. True, the high priest delivered Jesus to Pilate for trial but that was not done by the will of the *Jewish people*. Political conditions which prevailed at that time in Judaea forced some of the leaders to fight against their own brethren, and to help the Romans to destroy the real Jewish patriots."

It is in such words that Solomon Zeitlin, head of the Rabbinical Department at Dropsie college, in Philadelphia, concludes his brilliant and scholarly study of "the most momentous event in human history" ("Who Crucified Jesus?" Harper). He says, "The trial and crucifixion of Jesus was the culmination and denouement of the whole dramatic struggle that gave birth to a new faith for mankind. This new faith wielded great influence not only on the life of its Christian devotees, but moulded the whole course of human civilization."

But the volume is more than merely a critical study of the single event of the crucifixion. It is, indeed, an extremely satisfying description of the social, economic, and political life of the Jews who lived under the procuratorship of Pontius Pilate, written by one of the most impressive Jewish scholars of the day. Dr. Zeitlin speaks of Jesus with the utmost respect and appreciation, of the New Testament record with eminent approval, and of the teachings of Jesus with genuine reverence.

Caiaphas, the high priest who was responsible for hailing Jesus before Pilate, was a quisling, thoroughly hated by the Jews and despised even by the Romans. The Sanhedrin which passed the judgment was a political clique, quite separate and distinct from the religious group, of the same name, which ruled in all spiritual matters for the Jews. The execution was justified by the Romans on the ground that Jesus was an insurrectionist who plotted a rebellion against the empire, and the Christian church for 20 years was believed by the Romans to be a seditious organization.

All this Dr. Zeitlin explains with minute care and convincing scholarship. And his evidence should be studied with great respect by every preacher and teacher of the Christian gospel. This is an extremely illuminating and important book.

This editorial published in an official organ of one of the foremost orthodox churches in this country shows sincere goodwill towards the Jewish people, and was the first step taken by an orthodox church to remove the stigma from the Jews that they had crucified Jesus.

In this as well as in other countries many Christians, both Catholics and Protestants, in order to combat anti-Semitism, have organized societies of goodwill toward the Jews and declaimed against religious bigotry and racial hatred. They certainly do help to establish a better relationship between Christians and Jews. We must not forget, however, that even the minister of the gospel no matter how well intentioned in preaching in the church goodwill toward the Jews, does preach and teach on solemn occasions that the Jews crucified Jesus. This is done especially during the Holy Week and on Easter. This is taught in the schools to the children; thus the minds of the children have already been poisoned in the schools, and no sermon of goodwill by Christian or Jew could be an antidote to this poison. I strongly doubt whether goodwill organizations and anti-defamation societies can eradicate anti-Semitism. The Jews have been defamed too long.

The question then confronts us: can anti-Semitism be eradicated? The answer is: yes, it can in time, if the Christians are really interested in combating it. I do not mean that textual emendations or changes should be made in the New Testament with respect to the crucifixion of Jesus. The New Testament is holy for the Christians as the Hebrew Bible for the Jews. What I hold is that the Apostles' Creed, which was recited in the early days of Christianity and is still recited in many Protestant churches, should be introduced into the schools. It is not stated in this Creed that the Jews crucified Jesus.

Pius XI, in one of his encyclicals said, "In spirit we are all Semites." In introducing the Apostles Creed in the schools, Church leaders would perform an act of goodwill to the Church and to its Jewish mother religion.

The idea of super-nationalism has always implied the separation of one people from another. Nations have fought one another throughout history down to our day. More than two thousand years ago the Prophet Isaiah had a vision that the time would come when no nation would raise the sword against any other nation. This prophecy is far from being fulfilled; however, in our own time the best minds of every nation are studying the means of preventing war between fellow men. For this purpose the United Nations was established in which nations have been taking part, in order to reconcile their differences not by the sword, but by justice.

When in ancient times nations had their national gods, they believed that their gods fought in their battles for them. When a nation was a victor, the god was the victor. When a nation was vanquished, the god was taken into captivity. Judaism and Christianity—and other universal religions—fought against the idea of national gods. They hold that there is only one God, the Father of all humanity. Judaism and Christianity both have fought against maintaining distinctions between nationalities and races. All are children of the Creator. There is no difference between people of one race and those of another before God. He is the Supreme Being of the entire universe—The Creator of all mankind.

It may still be a dream to have a *league* of all universal religions to work for the equality of mankind and brotherhood of humanity, but some day this dream may be realized.

SOLOMON ZEITLIN

September, 1955
Dropsie College

CHAPTER I

PROBLEMS

THE crucifixion of Jesus was a momentous event in the history of humanity. It influenced every aspect of Western civilization and culture—philosophy, music, literature, painting, art and architecture; it affected all phases of the social, political and economic life of society. More than his birth, the crucifixion of Jesus was responsible for the nature and growth of Christianity. Paul, in his letters to the Corinthians and to the Galatians, as well as the early Church Fathers laid greatest stress upon the crucifixion, asserting that through his blood an everlasting covenant was made with his followers. The early Church Fathers portrayed Jesus as the Paschal Lamb that was sacrificed to redeem the world from Eternal Sin.

So much more emphasis was placed upon the crucifixion than upon the birth of Jesus that the date of his birth is not given in the Gospels. Paul did not record it. Neither the Apostolic Fathers nor the ante-Nicene Church Fathers mentioned the twenty-fifth of December as the date of Jesus' birth. The Eastern Church celebrated the Nativity on the sixth of January together with the Festivity of Epiphany. To our own day the Armenian church celebrates the sixth of January, the Festivity of Epiphany, with greater solemnity than December twenty-fifth, Christmas. Indeed, not until the end of the fourth century was December

twenty-fifth first recognized as the date of the Nativity.
Thus, from the very beginning, the crucifixion has held
a fixed and definite place in the long epic of Christian
experience.

Jesus was by birth a Jew. Nowhere in the Christian
literature is this denied; on the contrary, many inci-
dents and passages in the Gospels affirm his Jewish
birth. He is portrayed as a descendant, by flesh and
blood, of the royal family of David. The Gospels of
Matthew and Luke trace his genealogy directly from
King David. Matthew recorded that, when the three
Wise Men of the East came to Jerusalem, they inquired, "Where is he that is born King of the Jews?"
Matthew continued to narrate that, when Herod heard
about this, he gathered the chief priests and the scribes
and asked them to tell him, "From where Messiah
(Christ) should be born?" When Jesus stood before
Pilate, Pilate asked him, "Art thou the King of the
Jews?" and Jesus replied, "Thou sayest." And when
he was crucified, the words "Jesus, the King of the
Jews" were inscribed in Greek, Roman and Hebrew
on the cross. Thus, we learn from the Gospels that
Jesus was a Jew, a descendant from the seed of David,
and was crucified as a Jew.

Yet, the Jews were accused of crucifying Jesus. It is
natural to ask why would they do it? What sin had
Jesus committed against the Jews or against their religion that they should crucify him? Some scholars place
responsibility for the crucifixion on the Sadducees, one
of the powerful Jewish sects of that day. By this reason-
ing they sought to exonerate the Pharisees, the great

bulk of the Jewish people, from this reproach. But this shifting of responsibility for apologetic purposes could not absolve entire Jewry, since the Sadducees themselves were a part of the Jewish people. It is true they were a minority, the aristocratic element, but they were nevertheless, Jews. Moreover, there was only one Temple and one religious Sanhedrin of seventy-one members dominated by the Pharisees. If a Sadducee chanced to hold office in either, he was forced by public opinion to follow the doctrines of the Pharisees. Hence, there is no point in attributing the trial and the conviction of Jesus to the Sadducees.

The negative thesis of this book—that neither the Pharisees nor the Sadducees, i.e., the Jewish people, were responsible for the crucifixion of Jesus—is sustained by fresh examination of all the sources relating to the crucifixion of Jesus. We shall re-examine the Synoptic Gospels, the Apostolic Fathers, the *Tannaitic* literature, the writings of Josephus and the Roman historians. From these sources comes irrefutable proof that attributing the crucifixion of Jesus to the Jewish people is a cruel and libelous accusation against the Jews.

The question then arises why the Church throughout the ages has placed the blame of the crucifixion upon the Jews? Before this question can be fully answered, other matters relevant to the tragic rôle of Jesus in the complexity of Jewish-Roman relationships must first be made clear. Such questions as Jesus' descent from Davidic origin, the meaning of his numerous conflicts with the Pharisees, the rôle of the Sanhedrin in the Second Jewish Commonwealth—all these are vitally important and require elucidation.

For example, why did the Synoptic Gospels lay such stress on the point that Jesus was a scion of the family of David? Even the Gospel of John, who did not give the genealogy of Jesus, affirmed that "Messiah—Christ cometh of the city of David." Peter asserted that "God had sworn with an oath to him (David), that of the fruit of his loins according to the flesh, he would raise up Messiah (Christ) to sit on his throne." Similarly, Paul wrote "of this man's (David) seed hath God according to His promise raised unto Israel a Saviour Jesus." Furthermore, Paul, in his second letter to Timothy, wrote "Remember that Messiah (Christ) of the city of David was raised from the dead." Ignatius, among the Apostolic Fathers, referred to Jesus as one "who was of the family of David." In a word, all the Apostles and the Apostolic Fathers maintained that Jesus was a descendant of the family of David. What was the importance of David to the Jews during the Second Commonwealth? Who among the Jews believed that Jewish life would be established under a scion of David?

Again, we know from the Gospels that Jesus engaged in many arguments and controversies with the Pharisees. Why these conflicts? Paul asserted of himself that he was a Pharisee, the son of a Pharisee. Then why did Jesus have so many bouts with them? Who were the Pharisees? What rôle did they play in the development of Judaism up to and in the time of Jesus? Moreover, though the Jews never applied crucifixion as a penalty, for it was a Roman not a Jewish procedure, a Sanhedrin was convened, according to the Gospels, to try Jesus before he was put to death by Pilate. What part did the Sanhedrin play in this epic tragedy? What kind of institution was the Sanhedrin that tried Jesus?

The life of Jesus and his crucifixion were interwoven with the history of the Jewish people. Hence, to understand the events which led to his crucifixion and to establish the actual responsibility for this act, we must reconstruct the background in history of the Jewish people up to the time of Jesus. We must describe the parties and the institutions he knew and had contact with. We must also portray the political, religious and social life of the Jews among whom Jesus lived and died.

CHAPTER II

FROM THEOCRACY TO COMMONWEALTH

THE trend of Jewish history from the days of Ezra to the times of Jesus can best be seen in the struggle to recast the nature of the Jewish state from that of a theocracy in which the high priest ruled to that of a commonwealth in which secular leadership held the reins of government. It is only in terms of this struggle that much that transpired among the Jewish people during those crucial centuries can be understood properly. It was the proclamation of Cyrus of Persia, issued about 538 B.C., that launched the problem of leadership together with the restoration of the Jewish state.

1. THE RESTORATION AND THE DAVIDIC DYNASTY

The Biblical Book of Ezra tells dramatically how King Cyrus issued his proclamation to the Jews, bringing their exile to an end.

Thus saith Cyrus king of Persia: All the kingdoms of the earth hath the Lord, the God of heaven, given me; and He hath charged me to build Him a house in Jerusalem, which is in Judah. Whosoever there is among you of all His people—his God be with him—let him go up to Jerusalem, which is in Judah, and build the house of the Lord, the God of Israel, He is the God who is in Jerusalem.[1]

To manage the migration and execute the Restoration, the Crown chose or appointed two men. These two men were representatives of the two influential factions among the Jews—the royalty and the high priesthood. Zerubbabel, the grandson of Jehoiachin, formerly king of Judea, represented the royal family; Joshua, the grandson of Seraiah, represented the high priesthood. These two men shared together the responsibility of the establishment of the new community and the rebuilding of the Temple in Jerusalem. Soon, however, friction arose among the Jews as to whom leadership and the guidance of the new community should be entrusted.

Those who desired to organize the new community under the leadership of a secular authority as a political state wanted Zerubbabel to be sole leader as he was a scion of the royal family, a descendant of King David. Those, on the other hand, who were of the opinion that the reconstructed community should be organized on a religious basis maintained that Joshua, who came of priestly family, should assume sole leadership. The supporters of Joshua triumphed, and Zerubbabel disappeared as a political factor in the new community. Thus, Joshua became not only the high priest in the rebuilt Temple, but the sole leader of the new community.

Undoubtedly, the reason for the victory of the religious party lay in the strong belief that the Persian government would disfavor Zerubbabel as leader. The Jews feared that the Persian government would suspect Zerubbabel of ambitions to lead the Jews into revolt and set up an independent political state, since he was the grandson of King Jehoiachin of the Davidic family. Moreover, there was a likelihood that a large part of the new community were antagonistic to Zerubbabel, because many Jews attributed the calamities following the destruction of the Temple entirely to the policies of their former kings. Therefore, they did not want any descendant of this royal family as leader. Thus, the new Jewish community, after the return from Babylonia, was established under the authority of the priests.

Disquieted by the reports of unsatisfactory conditions in the new Judea, the Babylonian Jews besought King Artaxerxes' permission to send a mission there. The king granted this permission to Ezra, and enabled him to assume authority over the Jewish community in Judea. Ezra was a priest, a descendant of Zaddok,[2] the first high priest of the Temple built by Solomon.[3] In Ezra the king vested the power to appoint judges who were to instruct the people in the laws of God and the laws of the state. These judges had the right to punish transgressors of the laws of God or of the state by confiscation of goods, by imprisonment, or even by death. Subsequent kings of Persia conferred this authority upon later high priests. Thus, the new Jewish settlement was established as a theocracy[4] in which jurisdiction over the people was wholly vested in the high priests, who became the sole authorities over the Jewish people.

The Jews still in Babylonia also favored the theocracy rather than a community under the rule of a scion of the family of David. They had understandable reasons: they feared that, if their brethren in Judea should instigate a revolt against the Persian government, they would likewise be suspected. Moreover, they were certain that Ezra, being a priest who received his authorization from the king, would rule over the Jews both in accordance with the Jewish law and the laws of the Persian government; that is, in religious matters he would be guided by the Jewish law, and in civil matters he would be guided by the Persian law.

2. THE THEOCRACY AND THE CANONIZATION OF THE PENTATEUCH

The canonization of the Pentateuch is associated with the establishment of the theocratic state. It came about in this way. Ezra, having the responsibility of organizing the new Jewish state on a religious basis, proceeded to have eighty-five representatives of the Jewish community sign a declaration accepting the five books of Moses as divine revelation binding them forever. Ezra was thus instrumental in canonizing the Pentateuch; and together with this canonization, the theocracy became the established system of government in Judea.

But more was involved in the canonization of the five books of Moses than appeared on the surface; what was implied in it was the rejection of leadership by a scion of the family of David. In the Pentateuch, Phineas, the grandson of Aaron, received the priesthood as an eternal heritage for himself and his seed forever.[5] Later, in the blessing of Moses, Levi was designated not merely as a priest but also as a leader of his people, for Moses said that Levi and his descendants should teach the Law to the people and exe-

cute the judgments.[6] Thus, Moses designated Levi as
leader of the Jewish people. King David, on the other
hand, was in no way mentioned in the five books, even
by the slightest suggestion. It is true that Jacob in his
blessing exalted Judah, the progenitor of David,[7] but
Moses, the lawgiver, ignored Judah in his blessing and
ascribed leadership to Levi.

Although the Jewish state took the form of a theocracy after Zerubbabel disappeared from Judea, the
idea that a scion of the family of David should rule
over the Jews was not entirely obliterated from the
minds of the people. Many Jews still hoped that the
Jewish state would some day be ruled by a descendant
of the family of David. Especially among the lower
classes was this hope cherished. It was undoubtedly
due to this attitude toward the Davidic dynasty that
they and their leaders showed some opposition to the
high priests and to the theocracy.

By the canonization of the five books of Moses, the
Oral Law which was in vogue among the Jews for many
generations and the beliefs which the Jews cherished
were to be abandoned. The canon had a double purpose: to include those books which were considered
holy and to exclude those which were not deemed holy.
Those books and the common law which were not included in the canon were neither holy nor authoritative, and need not be followed. They were sometimes
even considered heretical.

The opposition of the people was not derived from
any doubt that the Pentateuch was given by God to
Moses. They preferred, rather, to believe that God gave

Moses many more laws which were not included in the Pentateuch: laws that were orally transmitted from generation to generation, laws that were of equal importance with those of the written law.[8]

It was from these oral laws that they derived the validity of Davidic leadership over the Jewish people. Had not God promised King David that his descendants would rule over the Jewish people? This was an oral tradition which they held dear. It was, therefore, on the validity of the Oral Law and the prophetic books that they based their belief that the leadership of the Jewish people should be vested in one who was a descendant of the Davidic family.

The high priest, on the other hand, and all those of the higher aristocracy connected with him not only opposed the restoration of civil authority under a Davidic scion, but also strongly resisted the oral, or unwritten, law on which the movement for that civil authority was based. Fearing that their power would be curtailed and that the movement of the adherents of the family of David be strengthened, the high priest and the aristocracy fought against the recognition and acceptance of the Oral Law.

3. THE ORAL LAW, THE PHARISEES AND THE SADDUCEES

Out of this controversy over leadership in the Jewish state—a controversy reflected in the conflicting attitudes toward the Oral Law—came the sects, or parties, that distinguished that period of Jewish history.

The priests and the higher aristocracy called those who believed in the Oral Law as well as in the restora-

tion of the family of David, *Perushim*—Pharisees—
Separatists, that is, those who separated themselves from
the Jewish people and the Pentateuch. They held that,
because these Pharisees maintained that Jewish leadership should be vested in a scion of the Davidic family,
they stood in opposition to the Torah. They pointed
out that God had made a covenant with the priests
in the Pentateuch; nowhere is there mention made
of David; furthermore, God did not give Moses any
other laws than those in the Pentateuch. Therefore,
those who believed in the Oral Law were actually
defying the Pentateuch. On the other hand, the priests
called themselves *Zaddokites*—Sadducees, since they
were descended from the High Priest Zaddok who
lived in the time of Solomon. Moreover, Zaddok was
of the lineage of Phineas with whom God had made
a covenant that the priesthood should be an eternal
heritage for himself and his seed forever.

Thus, the name "Pharisee" was coined and used by
the Sadducees who resented the opinion that the Jewish state should be established under the leadership of
a descendant of the Davidic family, and who, at the
same time, maintained that the Oral Law should be as
authoritative as the Written Law. Hence, the name
Perushim—Pharisees—was actually a nickname, a term
of opprobrium and contempt. The scholars who la-
bored in and developed the Oral Law never referred
to themselves as *Perushim*, Pharisees, Separatists.[9] In
the long course of Jewish history, however, the name
which originally was coined as a term of contempt
became, by common usage, the name of those who

believed oral tradition equally as binding on the Jewish people as the Written Law of Moses. An analogous
example of the rise of nomenclature like that of the
Pharisees may be seen in the reform movement against
the Pope in the sixteenth century. The Catholics
called the reformers within the Church, those who
were antagonistic to the Pope, Protestants. Surely, in
the beginning these would-be reformers did not call
themselves Protestants; but, in the course of time, what
had been a term of opprobrium became the accepted
name of the new Christians, namely, the Protestants.
History is replete with examples of this nicknaming
propensity.

4. THE REIGN OF THE SADDUCEES AND ASSIMILATION

The high priests, the Sadducees, by virtue of the
canonization of the Pentateuch, held full authority
over the Jewish people. Thus, the reign of the Sadducees began. The edict of the Persian king to Ezra
strengthened their power over the community. By this
authority the high priests appointed the judges. Those
malefactors who transgressed the Jewish law were tried
according to the Pentateuchal laws, while those who
transgressed the state laws were tried according to Persian laws. The Pharisees, so far as we can learn, had
little influence in shaping the affairs in the new Judea;
indeed, we may surmise that their influence was nil.

As the Sadducees became more powerful, corruptive
influences began to penetrate their ranks. By 332 B.C.,
the Persian empire had crumbled under the advance
of the Macedonian forces of the mighty Alexander.

What would have happened had Alexander completed his conquests we cannot guess. But, with his sudden death in 323 B.C., his vast empire fell to pieces and was divided among his generals. Ptolemy seized Egypt; Seleucus ruled Syria. Judea lay geographically between these two powerful states. Ptolemy, to strengthen his hold upon Egypt, conquered Judea; the Seleucidian dynasty, basing its claim on the Treaty of 301, demanded Judea as part of its empire.[10] Thus, Judea, extremely valuable to both as a buffer state, was caught in the machinations and struggles of Syria and Egypt. The Ptolemies, fearing that the Seleucides would invade Egypt and snatch their kingdom from them, held Judea on their north as a protection; the Seleucides, apprehensive lest Ptolemy might ultimately invade Syria, determined to dominate Judea to their south.

For over a century the empires of Egypt and Syria warred with each other for possession of Judea, and most of the battles were fought in the hills and on the plains of unhappy Judea.

Wars always bring destruction and misery to the land and to the people where armies clash. But, bad as war is, it may serve a useful purpose if it awakens the national consciousness of a people. In the days of the ancient judges and, later, in the period of the first kings of Israel, outside enemies served to crystallize the national feeling. They helped to bring about the sense of national consciousness. In those stormy days of the new Judea, foreign antagonists wrought a new consciousness in the hearts and minds of the Jewish people. For the first time since the Restoration, the

Jews, because of the conflicts of the two empires, awak-
ened to their national position, and took active part in
seeking to improve their political status. Of course, the
Jewish people were divided in their opinions as to
what policy to follow. Some were inclined to believe
that annexation to Egypt would greatly benefit them,
others argued for annexation to Syria.[11]

Meanwhile, with the passing of Persian influence
and with the ascendancy of Hellenism, fundamental
changes were taking place in the inner life of the
Jewish people. During the Persian period, Judea was
a small colony enjoying religious autonomy, but shun-
ning political intrigues. In the Hellenistic period, the
national consciousness being stimulated, interest was
taken in political matters. In the Persian period the
Jews were wholly engaged in agriculture, and lived
in the hills surrounding Jerusalem; there was no commerce, and without manufacturing, there were no
artisans. The Hellenistic period saw radical changes
in the economic and social life of the community.
Commerce was stimulated by the emergence of Alexandria as the greatest seaport city on the Mediterranean.
Through commercial connections with Egypt, Judea
benefited greatly. Wealth began to accumulate in
Judea. Some of the members of the priestly family held
office as tax collectors for their Egyptian overlords.[12]

The close intercourse between the Jews and the
Egyptian court wrought significant changes in the cultural life of the Jews. The Greek language was brought
into Judea. Many of the higher aristocracy spoke Greek.
They even Hellenized their names. Jerusalem, which

up to the Hellenistic period was an obscure town, now became a prominent metropolis. The corruptive influence of assimilation began its evil work.

So Hellenized did many of these aristocratic Jews become that they were ready to relinquish their names as "Jerusalemites," and preferred to call themselves "Antiochenes" in the time of Antiochus Epiphanes.[13] They began to yield to grandiose visions of annexation with Hellenistic Syria. They believed that by making Judea a part of the Great Syrian Empire they would improve not only their own personal fortunes, but would also enhance the welfare of the country at large.

These assimilationists did not have free and easy sailing. They were strongly opposed by Jews of the middle class, especially the Pharisees. So strong did this opposition become that the Syrian government had to take cognizance of it.

In 171 B.C. Antiochus Epiphanes, learning that the Ptolemian army was about to assault Syria, marched with his army to the Egyptian frontier. Having met the menace firmly, Antiochus made his way back from Egypt. He invaded Jerusalem, entered the Temple, and slew many Jews who were known to be opposed to the Hellenization of Jerusalem.[14]

Judea was very important to Antiochus politically. Since the loss of Asia Minor to the Romans, the Mediterranean coast of Lower Syria had become of paramount importance to the Syrian government. Antiochus, therefore, strove desperately to retain Lower Syria including Judea. He determined to eliminate whatever Jewish opposition there was to his schemes.

He was convinced that he could not completely depend upon the Hellenistic party in Judea; therefore, he decided to destroy the Jews in Judea by force. He began his plan by prohibiting the Jews, on threat of punishment by death, from keeping their laws.

He dedicated the Temple itself to Zeus Olympus. He built a new fortress on Mount Zion. He set a body of royal troops, the Macedonians, in the city to dominate it.[15] By these means, Antiochus thought he would destroy Judaism and make Judea a colony of Syria.

In all this Antiochus was aided and abetted by the Hellenistic party led by the high priest, Menelaus. These Hellenistic Jews played the same rôle in Judea that the Fifth Column has played in modern Spain and Norway and other outraged countries of our times. They helped Antiochus to conquer Jerusalem. But most likely they, like their modern counterparts, later suffered disappointment through the policy of Antiochus. They thought that they would be able to make Jerusalem a Greek *polis*, and thus that they themselves would become citizens of the Great Syrian Empire— "Antiochenes of the city of Jerusalem." Their plans were completely frustrated. The city was reduced to a mere colony. The high priest, Menelaus, was relegated to the position of a gendarme, a "Quisling" in our parlance, for Antiochus. He was instructed to see that the Jewish law should not be observed and that anyone who observed the Jewish law, and thereby disobeyed Antiochus' orders, should be put to death. To these depths of degradation did the assimilationist policy of the ruling Sadducees bring the Jewish people.

5. REVOLT AGAINST ASSIMILATION AND THE ESTABLISH-
MENT OF THE COMMONWEALTH. TEACHINGS
OF THE PHARISEES

A violent reaction mounted against the forcible Hellenization of the Jews by the puppet high priest. The Jews defied Antiochus' orders. They observed the Sabbath and circumcised their children. Those who were caught were tortured and put to death. But these repressive measures only added fuel to the flames of revolt.

A new group appeared in Judea called *Hasidim*— the Pietists. In the face of grave danger, they insisted upon observance of the Jewish law. Despite the fact that their infants were often murdered at their mothers' breasts, they circumcised them. Many episodes of hero-ism and martyrdom are recounted of these Pietists. The author of the Second Book of the Maccabees nar-rates how a group of Jews hid themselves in a cave in order to observe the Sabbath. When the agents of Antiochus discovered them, they threatened them with burning unless they profaned the Sabbath. The Pietists refused, and were burned to death.[16]

The same author relates another episode whose tragic heroism is unforgettable in the annals of civili-zation. The officials of the king arrested seven children together with their mother for observing the Jewish law. On command they refused to profane the re-ligion of their forefathers, choosing death instead. The king, in order to compel their submission, ordered that they should all be present when each was tortured.

But, regardless of their great agonies of body and mind at the cutting off of limbs and burning by hot fires, they preferred death rather than submission to the king.[17]

These *Hasidim* met the edicts of Antiochus with the silent scorn of nonresistance. They were *the first martyrs in history*. For they died in order to bear witness (martyr) to the truth of their religion. Through their deaths, they protested against superstition and religious persecution.

For a time it appeared as if Antiochus had triumphed over the Jews. Momentarily Judaism seemed to have been defeated by a paganistic Hellenism. The situation was black, indeed. The Hellenistic party had become the agents of Antiochus and executed his orders ruthlessly against Jews loyal to their faith. The *Hasidim*, concerned only with spiritual resistance, had 'no interest in the larger political interests of their people, and did not deem it worthwhile to resist Antiochus by force of arms.

Had there been only these two groups in Judea, the Jews would have disappeared and Judaism would have been extinguished as a religion from the face of the earth. And with them Christianity itself might never have come into being. Fortunately for civilization, another group of Jews matured at this time into active resistance against Antiochus and his hirelings. It was this group that won its way to strong leadership politically and militarily and saved Judaism, and, in the process, transmuted the nature of the Jewish state.

The beginnings of this movement were indeed humble. A lesser priest named Mattathias of an obscure family called Hasmonean dwelt in the little village of Modin. He and his sons saved Judaism and civilization by revolting against the Syrians. They sought not only to defy the king's decrees but actually used force against the officials of Antiochus. Mattathias and his five sons won the allegiance of the people at large into whose ranks Hellenistic culture did not penetrate. They were the people who resisted the forces of assimilation.

Among these people at large, the teachings of the Pharisees had made great strides. Indeed, the Pharisees won numerous recruits to their interpretation of Jewish life. Their resentment grew hot and strong against the high priests—the *Zaddokites*—who had forsaken the Jewish religion and had adopted the Hellenistic way of living. Two Pharisaic doctrines in particular strengthened them in their convictions to resist their enemies, foreign and domestic.

The first doctrine concerned the leadership of one of Davidic dynasty; it was a doctrine which at that time promised to unify the scattered and divided forces of the Jewish people. In Hellenistic times most of the Jewish people still lived in Babylonia, while only some of them lived in Palestine. The Pharisees taught that God would some day unite the Jewish people under the scepter of the family of David. This hope kindled the imagination and high determination of the people. So strongly did this hope work in the hearts of the people that even some of the priests were influenced by it. Ben Sirah, in his *Ecclesiasticus*, although a priest himself, wrote of King David: "And He gave him (David) the Covenant of Kings and the throne of the glory of Israel."[18]

Mattathias, in his testimony to his sons, also affirmed that, while the priesthood was given to the family of Phineas, the kingdom was given to David forever and ever.[19] This doctrine that the Davidic dynasty would be re-established spread in favor among the rank and file of the people. Its popularity is attested to in the psalms which were read by the people who were, in turn, strengthened by those psalms. For in the psalms, sung by the Levites in the Temple, David was represented as the Jewish king, the king of the humble and the poor. One of these psalms asserted that God made a covenant with David that his children would sit upon the throne of Israel forever and ever. And in this psalm David was called "My Anointed," that is, "My Messiah—My Christ."[20]

The second doctrine of the Pharisees which inspired the life of the Jewish masses with hope and daring was concerned with the matter of reward and punishment in the future world, and resurrection. The significance of this doctrine lay in its motivations in the hearts of the people here and now. It helped to answer questions concerning God's justice in a world that seemed filled with injustice. It renewed their faith sufficiently to enable them to struggle with high hope that their reward was assured, if not in this world, then surely in the world in which God's justice comes to its complete fulfillment.

Many wondered then, as many wonder now, why people who meticulously observe the precepts of God should suffer, while the wicked enjoy a prosperous life. The Pharisees taught that reward and punishment do not refer to the body but to the soul. Thus, the soul of the righteous in the future world would enjoy immortality; but the soul of the wicked would suffer punishment in the life after death. This doctrine gave meaning to the sufferings and struggles of the ordinary people of Israel. It gave them strength and courage in their sufferings, for they hugged the hope in their hearts that some day they would be rewarded for their good deeds. The teaching of the Pharisees that the righteous man would be resurrected captivated the imagination of the simple people. They cherished the dream that some day they would enjoy everlasting life.

This doctrine of resurrection re-enforced the courage of the Jews to resist the Syrians. They fought the enemies of their religion fearlessly like lions, believing, nay, convinced that God would reward them and grant them eternal life. The author of the Second Book of the Maccabees describes how the Martyr Brethren, while they were being tortured by the Syrians, said to the king that they were ready to die, for God would raise them up to everlasting life.[21] And they met death without fear. The torture did not penetrate to their souls. They were happy, for they looked forward to meeting their Master, Almighty God, who would reward them by resurrection. Moreover, they were convinced that the wicked Antiochus would be brought to judgment and made to suffer eternal misery in the world hereafter.[22]

Mattathias, in his attitude toward fighting on the Sabbath, was undoubtedly influenced by the Pharisaic attitude toward a necessary profanation of the Sabbath for the saving of human life. The Pharisees taught that, to save a human life, it is permitted to violate the Sabbath, because they held it is better to profane one Sabbath in order to make it possible for the person saved to observe all the Sabbaths that lay in the future.[23] In this Mattathias was unlike the *Hasidim*, the Pietists, who let themselves be burned alive without any resistance. Mattathias urged the use of force in opposing the king and his cohorts. He even issued an order to his followers that, if they were attacked on the Sabbath, they should make use of arms notwithstanding the sanctity of the Sabbath.[24]

When Mattathias died, his sons took over the leadership in the struggle against the Syrians. Through the military victories of Judas Maccabeus and the political statesmanship of his brothers, Jonathan and Simon, the Jews gained their independence. In the year 142 B.C. an independent Jewish state was proclaimed. A great assembly convened, consisting of Israelites, Levites and priests. They elected Simon, the son of Mattathias, to be high priest and ruler over the newly established state.[25]

Simon was entrusted with the high priesthood and secular leadership as a heritage for his children with the proviso, "until a true prophet should arise in Israel." This honor was accorded him and his family in recognition of their heroism and self-sacrifice on behalf of the

Jewish people. They, through their bold courage even to the shedding of their blood, won Jewish independence.

Simon's appointment to the high priesthood was a revolutionary act in the life of the Jews. For centuries and centuries, the high priesthood had been held by one family, the *Zaddokites*, a descendant of Phineas with whom God, according to the Pentateuch, had made a covenant.

Now, for the first time, an ordinary priest of humble extraction became high priest. Moreover, the early high priests of the Zaddokite family enjoyed their position by virtue of being descendants of Zaddok, the high priest. They ruled over the people by the authority of the Pentateuch. They did not need the consent of the people.

Simon was elected to the high priesthood by a great assembly of the people. The high priesthood was given to him by the people. He now ruled by reason of the power delegated to him by the people, in recognition of his statesmanship. So popular was the idea of a restoration of the Davidic dynasty with the people that, when they elected Simon to be high priest and ruler, they made the important condition that it would be entrusted to him to the time "when a true prophet should arise."

Thus, by the election of Simon, the theocracy, which had been the form of government in Judea from the time of the Restoration under Ezra, was abolished and a commonwealth was established.

6. THE REIGN OF THE PHARISEES AND THE DEMOCRATIZATION OF JUDAISM

Before the Maccabean period, state authority was entirely in the hands of the high priests and the aristocratic families who were the *Zaddokites*, the Sadducees. The Pharisees had no actual power in the state; they were, however, a potent influence among the masses. After the establishment of the independent state through the victory of the Hasmoneans, made possible by the support given them by the Pharisees, the Pharisees gained important power, and their reign can be said to have begun.[26] They immediately sought to democratize the institutions of Jewish life, and endeavored to bring the Jews into direct contact with the Temple service.

Before the revolt of the Hasmoneans, Jewish religious life was concentrated in the hands of the priests; the Israelites did not participate in the ceremonies which took place in the Temple. After the establishment of the commonwealth, when the Pharisees became a force in Judea, they endeavored to make the Jewish religion not only a state religion but an individual religion, by encouraging Israelites to participate in the religious ceremonies as well as the priests.

The democratic attitude of the Pharisees toward the Temple service revealed itself, for example, in such important matters as the "Daily Sacrifices" and the institution of the *Maamadot*, the "Communal Divisions."

According to the Biblical law, sacrifices were brought to the Temple every day, morning and afternoon. The

Sadducees who consisted of the wealthy classes and who sought to monopolize the Temple by devising means of excluding the masses, opined that the daily sacrifices should be considered as private matters so that any individual who wished to do so should provide the lamb slaughtered in his name.[27] Only the rich could afford the luxury of this sacrifice. The wealthy man could either bring a lamb for the daily sacrifice or offer to the Temple treasury the necessary money for purchasing it.

The Pharisees, on the other hand, were of the opinion that the daily sacrifices should not be considered the concern of the individual, but should be provided by the entire Jewish community. The money for the purchase of the cattle should be supplied by the entire Jewish community, and not by individuals. It was in this spirit that they instituted the law that the animals should be purchased out of the funds of the Temple treasury to which each Jew contributed his equitable portion.[28] Hence, the Jewish people as a whole would participate in the Temple service.

But this did not entirely satisfy the democratic intentions of the Pharisees. They sought more than a reform of the manner of providing the daily sacrifices out of communal funds. They wanted the entire people actually to participate in the ceremonial slaughtering of the daily sacrifice in the morning and afternoon. To this end they instituted the following arrangement: The Israelite inhabitants of each city, town and village were divided into twenty-four divisions called *Maamadot* (Communal Divisions). The members of each *Maamad* were to go to the Temple to take part in the ceremony of the slaughtering of the daily sacrifice. Together, the members of these Communal Divisions represented the entire Jewish people. But, not all Israelites of the division could go or wished to go to Jerusalem. Therefore, it was arranged that the members who remained at home gathered in their respective cities and towns on the days on which they were supposed to be in Jerusalem, and read portions of the Pentateuch relating to the sacrifices. From this institution of the *Maamadot* the Synagogue developed. Since the Synagogue is the mother of the Church, it is logical to say that the origin of the Church may also be traced back to the *Maamadot*.[29]

Further insight into the democratic nature of the Pharisees can be obtained from their controversies with the Sadducees over such matters as the elimination of caste distinctions among the people, and the applicability of Pentateuchal law to the changing needs of life. These controversies are recorded in the *Tannaitic* literature.

Concerning caste distinction. According to the Bible no work may be done on the Sabbath. However, sacrifices were brought to the Temple on the Sabbath, and the priests performed their duties in slaughtering the sacrifices on the Sabbath day. Surely this was "work." Yet, this was not considered work that profaned the Sabbath. Why then should an ordinary Israelite be forbidden to gather in barley for his *Omer*, "a sacrifice of the first harvest of barley," on the Sabbath because this

constituted "work"? Why should there be such distinctions between priest and Israelite?

The Pharisees maintained that if, in the Temple, a
priest may work on the Sabbath because he is performing a religious service, an Israelite may likewise be permitted to work on the Sabbath if the work is for a religious purpose. The Pharisees, for example, permitted
the Israelites to reap the *Omer* on the Sabbath day,
if it fell on the 16th day of Nisan.[30] Apropos of this
point a very interesting story is told in the Mishnah
Menahot.[31] Once the 16th of Nisan fell on the Sabbath. The farmers reaped the barley on that day in
order to bring an *Omer* to the Temple. The Mishnah
continues the narration. "Is today the Sabbath?" asked
the farmers. And the answer returned was, "Yes." Then
they inquired, "May we reap today?" The answer returned was, "Yes." This was repeated three times to
demonstrate that, although it was Sabbath, work was
permitted since its purpose was religious. In this way
the Pharisees strove to eradicate caste differences which
were in vogue among the Jews of that period.

Law in consonance with life. The storm center of
the controversies between the Pharisees and the Sadducees is found in their attitudes toward the applica-
tion of the Biblical law to life. The Sadducees
demanded rigid observance of the Pentateuchal law.
The Pharisees, however, were ready to amend the
Pentateuchal law in order to bring religion into consonance with life. For the Pharisees, the Law was always
plastic; and they were acutely aware of the need to
modify the Jewish law in order to enable the Law to

accord with the requirements and demands of an ever-changing life. The following three cases suffice to reveal the liberalizing tendency of the Pharisees.

The laws of the Sabbath. According to the Bible, no Jew was allowed to go out from his "place" on the Sabbath, "abide ye every man in his place."[32] The word "place" was already translated in the Septuagint to mean "house." "You should sit each of you in your house."

To make the laws of the Sabbath less burdensome, the sages declared that the Jew had the right to walk from his house or from any other place which he had made his abode on the eve of Sabbath a distance of two thousand cubits. The Pharisees further interpreted the word "place" to mean city, and applied the principle of two thousand cubits to refer to the city.[33] Thus, a Jew had the right to walk two thousand cubits outside of the city limits on the Sabbath. That was called a "Sabbath day's journey."[34]

The Pharisees always had in mind to make the Sabbath a delightful day, a day of enjoyment, not a day of self-denial and grief. Thus, they instituted the law of Erub, which was a symbolic act by which the legal fiction of physical continuity was established. If a person deposited certain food at a definite place for the Sabbath or holyday, by this act he transferred, as it were, his abode to that place. Hence, from that place he might walk on the Sabbath two thousand cubits farther. To the Pharisees the Sabbath had been instituted for men and not men for the Sabbath.[35] For them the Biblical law "Remember the Sabbath day to keep it holy" described the Sabbath day as a day of enjoyment. "Call the Sabbath a delight," said the Prophet Isaiah.[36] For them the Sabbath was always a day of pleasantness. One New Testament scholar sententiously observed that "our blue Sundays" are no bequest from the Synagogue (Pharisees).[37]

The second case refers to ritual uncleanness. According to the Bible, if a person became ritually unclean, the mere bathing of the body in water was not sufficient to render the person ritually clean. He had to wait until sunset to complete his cleansing.[38] This worked great hardship on the Jews of that period, as it hampered them in their daily social life. The Pharisees, therefore, amended the Biblical law concerning impurity. They explained that the Pentateuchal law which stated that a man who was unclean must wait until sunset, referred only to the priests in the matter of eating their sacred food, the *Terumah*.[39] In the course of their ordinary life and social activities, mere washing of the body sufficed to render a person ritually pure, and it was not necessary to wait until sunset. Even this prerequisite of washing the body might, under certain circumstances, entail hardship, and the Pharisees, therefore, modified even this law by instituting the washing of the hands as a sufficient substitute to render the person ritually clean again.[40]

The third case was concerned with the Pentateuchal law which stated that, if water was put upon seed, the seed became susceptible to ritual uncleanliness.[41] The law made no distinction between seeds attached to the soil and seeds detached from the soil. This law was of great importance to an agricultural community, or to a community that imported grain from foreign lands. This law, if applied, would have made it impossible for the Jews in Judea to use the grain imported from Egypt, since the Egyptians irrigated their fields which would make the seeds susceptible to ritual uncleanliness.

The Pharisees, therefore, interpreted the word "seed" in the Pentateuch to mean only seed detached from the soil. Only such seed upon which water was poured was considered susceptible to uncleanliness. To the seed, however, which was attached to the soil this law did not apply.[42] With this interpretation, the Pharisees made possible the importation of grain by Jews from the rich granaries of Egypt.

This liberal interpretation of the Pentateuchal law was crucially vital to the Jews of Judea. From history we know that Judea suffered frequently from poor harvests, and often endured years of famine. Egypt was the granary of the Near East. Permitting the Jews of Judea to import food from neighboring Egypt was a great boon to the economic condition of the people. Many a time during the Second Commonwealth lives were saved by this imported grain, which otherwise would have perished from poor harvests and famines.

CHAPTER III

FROM COMMONWEALTH TO ROMAN PROVINCE

THE Commonwealth, which was established after the Jews won their independence on the battlefield, did not last long. Only a few decades after the Great Synagogue, representative of the people, had chosen Simon Hasmonean as the high priest and ethnarch, a monarchy was set up in Judea, and the kingdom was usurped by Simon's descendants. The people were ruled by tyrannical kings.

1. THE END OF THE HASMONEAN DYNASTY

Judea, less than a century after the Jews had gained freedom from the Syrians, was again conquered by another expanding power, the Romans. And the independence they had won at the cost of blood and tears was once more lost. The Jews suffered much more under the iron heel of Rome than under the rule of the Ptolemies. Simon, who liberated the Jews from the Syrians, was assassinated by his son-in-law, Ptolemy, meeting a violent death through treachery. His son-in-law did this in order to secure for himself supreme power over the Jews; however, he failed and the son of Simon, John Hyrcanus, succeeded his father as high priest and ethnarch.[1]

The Pharisees, fighting with the Hasmoneans, had made Jewish independence possible. They became the rank and file of the new state. Previous to the victory of the Hasmoneans, though representing the interests of the poor and the middle classes, the Pharisees had had no influence in the management of the Temple or in the community. Judea was controlled by the Sadducees. After the victory, however, the Pharisees came into power in the newly established state. The Temple service and Jewish life were guided by the Pharisees. Despite the loss of their zealous, protestant spirit, the name, Pharisees, was one to be conjured with, and the great majority of the people, including the high priest, John Hyrcanus, followed their behests and teachings. The name remained, the essence had evaporated. But this state of affairs did not last long either.

John Hyrcanus conquered numerous districts in the neighborhood of Judea, to the north, south and east. He subdued the Samaritans, and destroyed Samaria. He seized Idumea to the south, and compelled the Idumeans to accept Judaism. He marched into the countries east of the River Jordan, and conquered the city of Medaba.[2] His policy of conquest, however, did not please the Pharisees, for they never favored the subjugation of other peoples. Moreover, they objected to forcible conversion to Judaism. Hence, a clash ensued between John Hyrcanus and the Pharisees. The antagonism between them sharpened when Hyrcanus decided to change the form of government by declaring himself king of Judea.

The Pharisees condemned such action. They themselves were the heirs of the men of the Great Assembly who had elected Simon as a ruler "until a true

prophet will arise from Israel." The Pharisees held fast
to the doctrine that the kingdom belonged to the family
of David, that some day the Jewish Kingdom would be
restored under the scepter of a scion of the family of
David.

To re-enforce their devotion to the Davidic dynasty,
they brought support from the Hebrew Prophets. Under
the guidance of the Pharisees, during the Maccabean
period, the books of the Prophets were canonized,[3] and
became a part of the Bible, second in importance only
to the Pentateuch. These prophecies, given in the name
of God, predicted that Israel would be restored under
the kingdom of the family of David. It was clearly
stated, in these books, that God had made an everlasting covenant with David that his seed should reign in
Israel. And David was called "the Anointed," i.e., the
Messiah.

When, therefore, John Hyrcanus declared himself
king, he directly transgressed against the very words of
God. The Pharisees could never consent to his act, for
they regarded John Hyrcanus as a conscienceless
usurper. In his turn, John Hyrcanus, thereupon, abandoned the Pharisees and joined himself to the Sadducees.
He forbade the Jews to observe the laws ordained by the
Pharisees.[4] The Pharisees and their influence forcibly
diminished, and again they became the subordinate
party in the Jewish State. They were shorn of the
privileges they had hitherto enjoyed. And the Sadducees, waxing in strength under the favored smiles of
Hyrcanus, ascended once more to power.

The Sadducees, it will be recalled, were those who,

before the Maccabean period, consisted of the high priestly family descended from Zaddok. They included also the upper classes whose interests were identical with those of the high priest. The upper classes, in the time of the Ptolemies, like the upper classes of other subjugated peoples who are ever ready to adopt the customs of their conquerors and become assimilated, were willing to adopt the Hellenistic mode of life. Moved by desire to enhance their financial well-being, the Sadducees readily compromised with their conqueror. During the war for Jewish independence, they had lost their entire wealth and influence to the Hasmoneans who then constituted the high priesthood. Now the Sadducees had the chance to come into their own again, and they seized the opportunity with avidity.

John Hyrcanus pursued a policy of foreign conquest. He thrust back the frontiers of Judea. He added, through his political maneuvers, such maritime cities as Joppa to his kingdom. Commerce made great strides forward in Judea, especially after he had conquered Samaria. The ancient caravan roads, leading through Galilee and Samaria to the Mediterranean coast, where the goods were shipped, brought great wealth to the country. A new aristocracy arose. This aristocracy consisted of the newly rich as well as the military caste which fought in the wars under the leadership of John Hyrcanus.

Although the new aristocracy did not consist chiefly of the descendants of the family of Zaddok, a very small fraction most likely belonging to this family inherited the name—Sadducees. They adopted the beliefs and policies of the old aristocracy of the Zaddokites. They accepted only the Pentateuch, but denied the Oral Law, the Tradition of the Sages.[5] They did not believe in such Pharisaic doctrines as reward and punishment, and resurrection. The name "Sadducees" became a label descriptive of all those who rejected the principles of religion as laid down by the Pharisees. The Sadducees also believed in a strong, nationalistic state, with imperialistic tendencies; and they declared their intention to conquer cities and countries in order to enlarge Judea. Opposing these aggressive tendencies, the Pharisees laid stress on religion rather than on the expanding power of the state.[6]

John Hyrcanus did not succeed in his plan to assume the kingship. He met strong opposition from the Pharisees. With the conflict arising a few years before his death, he did not have sufficient time to bring his intentions into full fruition. His son, Aristobulus, succeeded him.

Aristobulus, besides assuming the high priesthood, transformed the commonwealth into a kingdom. Aristobulus was the first to assume the crown.[7] He reigned one year, and then the priesthood and the kingdom passed on to his brother, Jannaeus Alexander.

The new king continued the policies of his brother and father. He launched new wars against neighboring states. His policies, also, met determined opposition from the Pharisees, and civil war broke out in Judea. Thousands of Jews on both sides were killed. Jannaeus ultimately won the upper hand. According to Josephus, six thousand Pharisees were mercilessly slaughtered, and eight thousand fled the country.[8] These numbers, undoubtedly, are exaggerations, but it is quite evident that many Pharisees met their death. A tyrannical government was set up in Judea.

Before Jannaeus died, he left the reins of his kingdom to his wife, Alexandra. In his testament to her, he told her not to fear either the Pharisees or the Sadducees. But he warned her against the "tainted ones," "the hypocrites" who performed wicked deeds and claimed rewards as if they were pious men.[9]

On her succession to the throne, Alexandra appointed her eldest son, Hyrcanus, to be high priest. She released all the Pharisees who had been imprisoned by her husband, and allowed those who had fled to return to Judea. She reversed all the policies he had pursued. Once again, the Pharisees gained power.[10] The nine years of her reign were marked by great prosperity. She did not launch any foreign wars except one, and that was when her younger son, Aristobulus, led a military expedition against Damascus. Before she died, she inducted her eldest son, Hyrcanus, into the kingship.

Immediately, fratricidal strife broke out between Hyrcanus and Aristobulus. A temporary truce was concluded between the two brothers whose terms arranged for Hyrcanus to abdicate in favor of his brother, Aristobulus. But the truce did not hold for long. A crafty man named Antipater, for selfish reasons and by unscrupulous methods, destroyed the pact between the brothers. Antipater, whose ancestry hailed from Idumea, was the father of Herod, later crowned king of Judea.

Antipater, called the Idumean, schemed to acquire supreme power in Judea.[11] His plan was to use Hyrcanus as a stepping-stone to achieve his ambitions. He plotted to entangle the two brothers with foreign powers. To this end, he induced the Arabs to intervene on behalf of Hyrcanus; and later he sought the intercession of the Romans. Utilizing the presence of Pompey in Damascus in the year 63 B.C., the quarreling brothers laid their respective claims before him. At the same time, a group of Jews came before Pompey and presented their pleas for the re-establishment of a theocracy in Judea. Although the theocracy had been abolished in 142 B.C., many Jews still retained the hope, as they told Pompey, that "the form of government which they received from their forefathers was that of subjugation to the Priest of that God whom they worshipped"[12] a form of government they desired should again be set up over them. Apparently, some Jews had never been reconciled to the idea of a secular or civil government.

Pompey was not slow to see his opportunity and to seek his own advantage. He recognized qualities in Aristobulus, as an independent and high-spirited personality, which would never permit him to be used as a pawn in the political game. Hence, Pompey favored the elder brother, Hyrcanus, who was indolent by nature. Pompey moved on to Jerusalem, and after a sharp struggle that lasted three months, the Romans captured the Temple Hill. This took place on the ninth of Tammuz, the early part of July, a fast day.[13]

Hyrcanus was given the office of high priest and ethnarch; he was not appointed king. Judea, thus, came under the control of the Romans. But it would be a mistake to assume that the civil war between the two brothers was altogether responsible for the destruction of the Jewish state. The civil war provided the fortuitous opportunity for the Romans to seize Judea. After the Romans had conquered Syria and Egypt, they had no alternative but to dominate Judea, a small country geographically, but very important strategically. The Romans were fearful lest a strong, independent government in Judea would make an alliance with their arch-enemies, the Parthians to the East, and frustrate their domination over Egypt.

Pompey had declined the request of those Jews who favored the re-establishment of the theocracy. Moreover, he did not make Judea a Roman province. This was due, undoubtedly, to the policy of the Roman Senate which preferred to dominate the countries they conquered with the help of native kings and princes, rather than rule themselves. The Senate had a dual purpose in this technique: to prevent the outbreak of revolts as much as possible, and to lessen the burden of heavy taxes upon the Romans. Moreover, the very proximity of Judea to Egypt militated against absorbing Judea into a province of Rome. Some time later, when Crassus proposed to annex Egypt, he was prevented from doing this by the Senate, and Julius Caesar was likewise forbidden by the Senate to take charge of Egypt. This is related by the Roman historian, Suetonius.[14] The same historian wrote that, when Julius Caesar became dictator, he did not make a province of it because "it might one day under a headstrong governor be a source of revolution."[15] Later Augustus Caesar never allowed any senator to enter Egypt without special permission.[16]

Between the conquest of Judea by Pompey and his defeat later by Caesar, civil war raged continuously in Judea. Aristobulus fled from Rome, where he had been taken prisoner, and waged war against Hyrcanus. Later his son, Alexander, struggled bitterly against Hyrcanus, his uncle. Caesar, after his victory, reappointed Hyrcanus as the ethnarch of the country, and gave him the high priesthood.[17]

The real ruler, however, was no longer Hyrcanus, but Antipater who had schemed all these machinations and fratricidal strife. Antipater became procurator, and his sons, Phasael and Herod, were made *strategoi*, governors, in Jerusalem and Galilee, respectively. Herod sought to please the Romans and to convert Galilee into a Roman country by killing off those who resented Roman domination, and who hated Herod himself as Rome's henchman.

Under the leadership of a man named Hezekiah, many Galileans organized themselves into small groups to fight the Romans. They had no organized army. They fought guerrilla warfare against their Roman conquerors, and against those Jews who had betrayed their fellow countrymen. The Romans called them "bandits" and "robbers," and Josephus used similar epithets to describe them.[18] However, they were in truth patriots, like those Macedonians who, before the First World War, fought the Turks, or, in our times, like the Chetniks in Serbia. Hezekiah and some of his followers were killed by Herod. This murderous act incensed the

Jews of Jerusalem against Herod. And they compelled the vacillating Hyrcanus to summon Herod to stand trial before the Sanhedrin. Herod escaped the death penalty, only through the intervention of Hyrcanus.[19]

Antigonus, the second son of Aristobulus, in the year 41 B.C., endeavored to regain the throne. With the help of the Parthians, he overpowered Hyrcanus who was taken captive. Herod, however, escaped to Rome, where the Roman Senate, acting on the advice of Anthony, proclaimed him king of Judea. In the year 38 B.C. on the twelfth day of January, the fast day of the tenth of Tebet, Herod, aided by the Roman army, captured Jerusalem.[20]

Thus, the Hasmonean dynasty came to an inglorious end.

2. THE REIGN OF HEROD

The reign of Herod, begun in bloodshed, ended with mock heroics and the pretense of national sorrow. It is a bloody and sordid tale—this tale of Herod who never overcame the inner guilt of his crimes, the gnawing sense of insecurity, the furious hunger for domination that sometimes drove him to insane lengths. If ever a dictator revealed the pathological roots of his drive for power, the inner emptiness of his claims for rulership, the futility of his aspirations for glory, the evil consequences of his momentary triumph through violence, treachery and death—that tyrant was Herod.

Herod, the son of Antipater, became king of Judea by the grace first of Anthony, and later, of Octavius Caesar. Herod's kingship over Judea was that of a *rex socius*, that is, he was entrusted with the kingdom only as long as he lived. After his death, the Emperor Augustus had the power to decide who should succeed him. When Herod sought to put his sons to death, he had to obtain permission from Augustus. Though he retained authority over his own people, he had no power to engage in foreign wars. Foreign policy was dominated by Rome. He could make no alliances and conclude no treaties. When Rome engaged in imperialistic wars, Herod had to supply auxiliary weapons for her armies. His right to coin money—a sovereign right jealously defended by rulers—was restricted. Ruling Judea only as long as he continued in the favor of Augustus, Herod was a vassal to his Roman overlord.

As his first act of kingly power, Herod, to forestall any revolution that might rise against him, put to death all the old aristocracy. The members of the Sanhedrin which at one time had tried him for homicide, he killed outright, all except one member, Sameas (Shemaiah).[21] Being a plain Israelite unable to perform the functions of the high priest, Herod appointed a member of a minor priestly family to that high position.[22] Herod was fearful of entrusting the high priesthood to the old aristocracy, hence he chose an ordinary priest for the position. The high priest now depended upon Herod's pleasure. To fasten a firmer grip upon the high priest, Herod even kept the priestly vestments under his own supervision.

Through the intervention of Anthony, Herod was compelled to appoint his brother-in-law Aristobulus to the high priesthood. Shortly after, through devious trickery of Herod, this Aristobulus, the son of Alexander, was drowned.[23] Herod, knowing that the Jews never became reconciled to him as king, yet desirous of winning their approval of him, resorted to two devices: he tried to win the people by building new cities, by improving their economic conditions. This gave employment to them, and also appealed to their sense of national pride. And, in times of famine, he bought produce at his own expense to feed the people. From time to time, he reduced the heavy burden of taxation. He rebuilt the Temple, making it a magnificent edifice. He declared himself the protector and patron of the Jewish people throughout the Roman Diaspora.

On the other hand, he introduced a spy system like that of the modern Gestapo. He did not permit Jews to gather together, to walk together, to eat together. His spies were stationed everywhere. He himself mingled among the people in disguise, to hear what they thought of him.[24] Whoever expressed any hostile thoughts, or openly criticized Herod was put to death in the most inhuman and atrocious manner. Most of those eliminated during his reign were the aristocracy, the Sadducees, and the late followers of the Hasmonean dynasty.

The Pharisees did not suffer as much as the Sadducees, for a fundamental change had come over them. Their grievous disappointments, their bloody conflicts, the confusions and alarms of the times, the harshness and cruelty of men tended to drive them from the world of realities, from the insincerities and hypocrisies of politics into a quietistic, other-worldly frame of mind. They who had shed their blood in the war for independence and the establishment of the commonwealth were a very embittered people. They had created a Frankenstein to their own hurt and a master to their undoing. By destroying the theocracy and bringing about the commonwealth, they regarded themselves as having made it possible for a Jannaeus Alexander to seize the government and establish a tyrannical monarchy. Still fresh in their memories were the atrocities which Jannaeus had inflicted upon them. The hundreds of thousands of Jews killed during the wars between the brothers for the ruling crown haunted the minds of the Pharisees.

Thus, provoked with their own early policy in bringing the commonwealth to birth, and, in reaction against their own misdeeds, they adopted a policy of *quietism*; they abandoned worldly politics and concentrated on religion. To such lengths did this rejection of an affirmative attitude to political realities go that, during the siege by Herod, Sameas (Shemaiah) and his disciple, Hillel, advised the Jews to capitulate.

Herod was aware of the animosity of the Pharisees toward the Hasmonean dynasty, hence he did not persecute them. And, when he compelled all the Jews to take an oath of allegiance to him, he absolved the leaders of the Pharisees, Hillel and Shammai, and their followers from taking such an oath.[25] However, those Pharisees who opposed him were mercilessly murdered. Thus, the quietism of the Pharisees conveniently fitted in with the violent policy of Herod toward his subjects.

As Herod's reign drew along, it was more and more

filled with cruelty, violence and bloodshed. More and more Herod revealed himself, through his schemes and his actions, as a psychopathic personality. He presented himself as tragic in his inner conflicts, conflicts between the desire for approval and the awareness of his failure to win that approval, between seeming conquest and the awareness of his failure to conquer. He did not gain the submission of the Jews, either by his terroristic acts against them or by the favors he conferred upon them. Like all dictators, he could not be satisfied by the mere conquest of the people; he wanted their acquiescence as well. This he never received. Stark frustration beset him until his mind reached the point of desperate madness.

Herod knew deep in his heart that he had reached his throne by murder, killing off the Hasmonean family. He was always fearful lest the Jews should revolt, and the kingdom be taken from him and returned to its rightful heirs. Thus, to obtain the security that ever eluded him, he went from murder to murder, but, like the illusory horizon, that final security continually escaped from his nervous grasp. He killed his brother-in-law, Aristobulus, whom he had been compelled to make high priest. He feared the very existence of Hyrcanus who lived as a captive in Babylonia, and he cunningly schemed to have him return to Jerusalem. Once returned, Herod accused Hyrcanus of treason. He produced a letter, undoubtedly forged, in which Hyrcanus allegedly asked the aid of an Arabian governor to restore him to his throne. On the basis of this flimsy evidence, Herod summoned a Sanhedrin and had the old king put to death.[26] Later, Herod killed his beloved wife, Mariamne, accusing her of adultery. Again, before a Sanhedrin summoned for the purpose, he set forth his accusation and had her put to death. A short while later, he had her mother, Alexandra, executed. Then, the blind compulsions that blindly drove him on, turned him against his two sons, and he accused Alexander and Aristobulus, the children of Mariamne, of plotting against their father. They, too, were brought before a Sanhedrin and were duly condemned to death by strangulation.[27]

A few days before his own death, Herod had another son, Antipater, killed. Thus the bloody stream flowed on, nor did it cease even with his own death. All were suspected by Herod of plotting to take the kingdom from him. While no doubt can exist of their fear and hatred of Herod, it is impossible to believe they all plotted against him. Only a deeper motive can explain Herod's orgy of inhuman murders. The tragic ghost of insecurity and guilt and frustration could not be laid, and Herod regarded members of his own family as symbols of living threats to his power. Determined to obtain their submission to his will, he was yet aware that nothing he did or could do would make them submit to him.

Josephus, in his account of the death of Mariamne, relates that, after she had been put to death, Herod seemed inconsolable, and cried and called her name incessantly. He even commanded a servant to call out her name, as if she were alive.[28] His agony of spirit has been immortalized in the words of Byron:

Oh Mariamne! now for thee
The heart for which thou bled'st is bleeding;
Revenge is lost in agony,
And wild remorse to rage succeeding.
Oh, Mariamne! where art thou?

The *Talmud* records a weird tale about Herod, that
he had her embalmed, and used to have carnal intercourse with her corpse.[29] If this story contains a germ
of fact, then Herod must have indeed become mad to
have fallen victim to necrophilia. Perhaps his relations
with her after death, if true, indicated not so much
necrophilia as an insane determination to bend her to
his will. For Josephus informs us that Mariamne, in
their physical relations, often refused to submit to
Herod.[30] A psychic make-up such as Herod's could brook
no independence, nor tolerate nonsubmission. Therefore, he sought from Mariamne in death what in life
he could not exact from her—complete submission to
his imperious will. What a strange commentary on the
insatiable nature of power that grows by what it feeds
upon but ever becomes more insatiable, until it de-
stroys itself in futility and consumes itself to ashes!

Even Herod's death did not stop the flow of human
blood. Shortly before he died, Herod summoned the
leaders of the Jews, and shut them up in the Hippo-
drome. In his dying words to his sister, Salome, he instructed her that these men should be put to death,
the moment he breathed his last breath.[31] His devilish
wish sought to associate his death with that of these
leaders, so that, in the common mourning, he also would
be mourned. He knew that the Jews never really ac-

cepted him as their King. He had ruled over them only by terror. He feared that after his death, they would not mourn him, indeed, they might even rejoice. Hence by killing the principal men of the Jews at the time of his own death, they would be mourned and the appearance of mourning in the homes of Judea might be construed as if it were for Herod. People would believe —such was his vain hope—and especially the Romans, that he, Herod, was being mourned by the Jews. His satanic scheme did not prosper, for, immediately after he died, his sister, Salome, freed all the Jews.

So great was the hatred of Herod and the desire for liberty that, at the mere rumor of his death, revolt was ready to break out. Such a false rumor did spread abroad just a few days before the actual passing of the king. And at once disciples of Judas and Matthias, acting upon the influence of these well-known Pharisees, tore down the golden eagle which Herod had erected over the gate of the Temple,[32] the hated image that symbolized the mastery of Rome over Judea, and the challenge of an impertinent paganism to the Jewish religion which abhorred images. When these men, including the leaders, were arrested and brought before the king, Herod inquired of them whether they did not know that such acts meant death. They replied that they were aware of the punishment, but that they believed that, for such noble acts, their souls would attain immortality and the reward of eternal happiness in the future world. They asserted that they had done their duty to avenge God's honor.

Subsequently, they were tortured with inhuman cruelty, and were finally burned alive. This episode revealed that, Herod, despite his terroristic acts, had not destroyed the spirit of the Jewish people. Moreover, not all the Pharisees had yielded to nonresistant quietism. The younger generation seethed with revolt against enslavement by Rome and its vassal, Herod. The winds of revolt were rising steadily, and heavy clouds darkened the horizons of Jewish-Roman relationships. The storm shifted from Judea to Galilee; and out of Galilee came Judas of Galilee and Jesus of Nazareth.

Herod made a last futile gesture in his will to keep the throne for his descendants. He designated Archelaus to occupy the throne of Judea, but Galilee he gave to his other children. Scarcely had Archelaus returned from the funeral, when riots broke out in Jerusalem. The rebellious leaders sent an embassy to Rome. They petitioned Augustus Caesar for the abolition of the monarchy in Judea and the re-establishment of a theocracy under a Roman protectorate.[33] Augustus was not yet ready or willing to make Judea into a Roman province. He still adhered to the Roman policy that vanquished countries be ruled by native princes under the protection of Rome. Thereupon Augustus confirmed the will of Herod and recognized Archelaus as the ethnarch of Judea. But Archelaus, soon banished by Augustus, did not rule for long.[34]

The Herodian nightmare came to a bitter end in bloodshed, torture, revolt and banishment.

3. JUDEA A ROMAN PROVINCE. THE PROCURATORS

Judea was declared a province of Rome to be ruled by a procurator with all judicial powers (*ius gladii*).[35]

The procurator resided in Caesarea, but, on the occasion of festivals, he came to Jerusalem where he lived in the palace of Herod. The main Roman army was stationed in Caesarea, but a cohort was quartered in Jerusalem.

From the time of Herod onwards, the high priesthood ceased to be hereditary. Herod had appointed and dismissed high priests whenever the occasion suited his purposes. Some of them did not even complete a full year in office. Now, since the procurator assumed the power to appoint the high priest, the latter was compelled to execute the orders of his superior. Thus he became a mere agent of the Roman authorities.

The assumption of complete power by the procurators made itself felt in every phase of Jewish life, religious as well as political. Herod, it was noted above, kept the vestments of the high priest under his control to symbolize his sovereignty over the priests. Now the procurators took over the supervision of the sacred vestments. Likewise, in the time of Herod, any Jew who was accused of a political offense like sedition or other offenses of a nonreligious nature was tried by a political Sanhedrin; and the king assembled a Sanhedrin to try such offenders from time to time. When Judea became a Roman province, the procurators assumed jurisdiction over political crimes. Trials were held and sentences passed by them. It was the duty of the high priests to take the malefactors to the procurator. They spied out and exposed those Jews who incited the populace against the Roman authorities.

Thus, the high priests were held responsible for the pacification of the country.

Some high priests became so thoroughly Roman in their sympathies that they wholeheartedly helped the procurators to destroy any opposition against the Romans. Other priests, however, were reluctant to be henchmen of the Roman authorities. To save their own lives, indeed, they had to comply with the severe rule of the procurators. The high priests who did not conform with the Roman policy of suppressing the Jews, were dismissed and punished. There remained some Jews, nevertheless, who never gave up the hope that some day their country would be resurrected as an independent state. These Jews incited the people to revolt against the Roman tyranny. The Roman procurators, as well as Josephus, called these people "brigands." They were, in truth, patriots who tried to undermine the Roman regime in Judea. They might well be compared to those French and Serbians who today secretly sabotage the German military machine. By their fellow citizens they are regarded as "patriots"; by the Nazis they are reviled as "brigands."

Upon Judea becoming a Roman province, the procurator decreed that a census be taken in order to fix the taxes to be levied on the Jews by Rome. The Jews raised strong opposition against the census and Judas of Galilee urged the people to revolt.[36] He appealed to them not to submit to Rome and not to accept the Romans as their rulers. God, he declared, was the one and only ruler of mankind. The taxes which were levied by the Romans were collected by publicans, tax collectors. The Jews despised these tax collectors as robbers who executed the policy of enslavement for the Romans. Pious Jews avoided any social contacts with these publicans.

The first procurator was Coponius (6 C.E. to 9 C.E.). He was succeeded by Marcus Ambibulus (9 C.E. to 12 C.E.) and Annius Rufus (12 C.E. to 15 C.E.). When Tiberius became emperor, Gratus was appointed procurator of Judea and was in office from 15 C.E. to 26 C.E. Gratus was followed by Pontius Pilate (26 C.E. to 36 C.E.).

Philo, describing Pilate, wrote that he was cruel by nature, and utterly lacked humane compassion. He resorted to robbery and oppression. He often sent men to death, untried in a court of law, and physically broken by all manner of cruelties.[37] Pilate especially disliked the Jews and their religious traditions. He went out of his way to flaunt his contempt for them.

It was, for example, a well-established custom that Roman soldiers, out of respect for the religious sensibilities of the Jews, never entered Jerusalem carrying standards with the image of the emperor on them. Pilate, however, to humiliate the people, ordered his troops to enter Jerusalem with their standards. The Jews refused to permit the soldiers to enter Jerusalem, though Pilate threatened them with annihilation. They were prepared to die, however, rather than permit this desecration.[38] The determined stand of the Jews compelled Pilate to withdraw his orders. It may be that this withdrawal was due to the fact that Emperor Tiberius followed the Augustinian policy of restraint from interference in the religious life of the Jews, rather than any consideration on the part of Pontius Pilate.

Of the atrocities that Pilate committed, the Gospel according to Luke, speaks with evident condemnation when it is concerned with the Galileans "whose blood Pilate had mingled with their sacrifices."[39] Pilate was unscrupulous in his dealings with the Jews. He was sly and treacherous. Once, when he undertook to bring water into Jerusalem, he used the sacred money of the Temple for this purpose. The Jews were indignant at this. When they came to him in large numbers and protested, he called out his soldiers and instructed them to carry their arms under their garments so that the Jews should be taken by surprise. After the Jews had laid their case before him, he signaled the soldiers to attack the Jews who were unarmed. Many Jews were killed.[40]

For ten years, Pilate piled crime upon crime in his antipathy for the Jewish people and their religion. Pontius Pilate was procurator of Judea when Jesus was crucified. Pilate was dismissed by the Roman government, and after him Marcellus (36 C.E. to 37 C.E.) was appointed. He was succeeded by Marullus (37 C.E. to 41 C.E.).

Judea was a veritable volcano ready to erupt. The scorn of the procurators for the Jews and their religion incensed the populace to continual outbreaks. Conditions became so aggravated when Emperor Gaius attempted to set up his image in the Temple that revolution threatened.[41] The rule of the procurators was marked by continuous disorders which culminated in the great war against the Romans. The Roman historian, Tacitus, confessed that Jewish patience could last no longer.[42]

Despite the acts and attitudes of the procurators against the Jews and their religion, which they considered gross superstition, it would be historically inaccurate to put upon them entire blame for the steady trend toward war between Judea and Rome. More was involved than merely corruption, treachery and cruelty of petty potentates who ruthlessly exploited a helpless people. There was a deeper basis for the growing antagonism between Jew and Roman, an antagonism rooted in different and conflicting ideologies. It was a conflict between Rome and Jerusalem, between the Jewish conception of the state and the Roman conception of the state. To the Jew, the state was subordinate to religion. Religion to the Jew was the supreme arbiter in the life of man. To Imperial Rome, religion was secondary to the state; the state was supreme. Therefore, an irrepressible conflict was in the making between the governors and the governed. The Jews considered the Romans not only as destroyers of their political independence but also as oppressors of their religion. The Romans, for their part, were deeply agitated by the stubborn resistance of the Jews politically as well as by their religious teachings about a universal God supreme over the state.

Suetonius relates that a belief prevailed all over the Orient that a leader would arise in Judea who would rule the world.[43] Other historians also recorded this prevailing belief.[44] It referred, of course, to the Jewish hope for the coming of the Messiah. This Jewish belief disturbed the Romans; they regarded it as a challenge to their own hegemony. Therefore, they viewed with alarm any Jewish movement against the Romans as a menace to their entire imperial dominance in the near East. They suppressed such movements with the utmost cruelty and rigor.

The procurators resorted to extreme measures to destroy anyone who proclaimed himself the Jewish king, Messiah. Not only did they destroy the man who claimed to be a prophet or a Messiah, but they also punished his followers severely. Suetonius also informs us that Emperor Claudius, otherwise friendly to the Jews, had the Jews expelled from Rome because he was disturbed by Jewish teachings concerning a Messiah who would rule the country, and because of the constant unrest due to the instigation of a *Chrestus* ("Christ, Messiah").[45]

When Claudius, after the assassination of Gaius, had become emperor of Rome, he raised his friend Agrippa to be king over Judea. This appointment of Agrippa was due not only to his personal friendship with Agrippa, but to political considerations also. The emperor believed that, by appointing a king of the Jewish faith, he would put an end to the disturbances. He sought to follow the policy of Augustus, namely, that it was more beneficial to Rome for a native prince to govern a vanquished country.

King Agrippa I ruled only three years, from 41 c.e. to 44 c.e. He died suddenly, and the cause of his death still remains a mystery. Did he die of natural causes, or was he poisoned by some of the Roman administrators?[46] It is possible that the latter is the true explanation. It was quite possible that Agrippa schemed to form a coalition of all the near-by vassal states against the Romans. This may be the reason why, after his death, Judea was again placed under a procurator.

After the death of Agrippa I, Fadus ruled as procurator of Judea for two years (44 C.E. to 46 C.E.). The appointment of Fadus kindled anew the flaming passions of the people against the Romans. Fadus, in order to exert his authority over Judea, did the one thing that exacerbated the anger of the people—he demanded that the sacred vestments of the high priest be placed under his control.[47]

In regard to these sacred vestments of the high priest, it must be emphasized that they had become, in the course of time, symbols of the power of king and procurator over the high priest; and the high priests, on their part, measured their independence in terms of their supervision over the priestly emblems. Herod was the first to have been entrusted with this power. Then King Agrippa I assumed this authority. Between these two kings, Judea had become a Roman province, the high priests were appointed by the procurators, and the procurators controlled the sacred vestments, for the high priests were entirely dependent upon the Roman rulers. After the demise of King Agrippa I, Judea was again ruled by a procurator, Fadus.

Emperor Claudius of Rome, acting on the advice of Agrippa II, King of Chalcis, did not hand over the sacred vestments to Fadus, as he had demanded. By this act Emperor Claudius curtailed the rights of the procurators, and the appointment of the high priests was no longer left in their hands. Henceforth, some autonomy was granted to the Temple priests. Moreover, the appointment of the high priest was returned to the Jewish ruler. In their political life, the high priests were responsible to the procurators, but, for their personal acts, they had to answer to King Agrippa II.

It is important for our purpose to point out that, from the time when Judea became a Roman province up to the reign of King Agrippa I (from 6 C.E. to 41 C.E.)—the years of Jesus' ministry and crucifixion—the high priests had been appointed by the procurators.

In the time of the procurator, Fadus, many anti-Roman attacks took place. A man named Theudas declared himself a prophet, and urged the people to rise in revolt against Rome. This prophet promised wonders to his followers—among them that the River Jordan would divide and let the people pass through. Fadus sent a Roman legion against Theudas. Many of his followers were captured and killed. Theudas himself was executed, and his head was sent to Jerusalem for exhibition.[48]

Apparently to calm the incensed Jews, Emperor Claudius appointed Tiberius Alexander, a Jew by birth, but a devotee of the Greek religion, to be procurator. He held this office from 46 to 48. The Emperor acted in the belief that, being a Jew by birth, Tiberius Alexander would exert strong influence on the Jews. But the choice proved unfortunate because the Jews, like any other people, hated renegades.

New revolts broke out against the Romans. Two sons of Judas, the Galilean, James and Simon, were arrested and crucified by Tiberius Alexander.[49] These brought on the removal of the procurator. He was succeeded as procurator by Cumanus (48 C.E. to 52 C.E.) whose administration was further marked by intense disorders and much bloodshed in Jerusalem, until Emperor Claudius had to remove him also.

Upon the advice of the high priest, Jonathan, the emperor now made Felix procurator (53 C.E. to 61 C.E.). Tacitus has drawn an unforgettable vignette of this slavish character. He states that Felix practiced every kind of deception, cruelty and lust, "using the power of a king with all the instincts of a slave."[50] Having influence in the court, Felix was confident that his misdeeds would be overlooked. His administration was marked by numerous horrors.

Many men were crucified, some of them openly, some by treachery. A man who hailed from Egypt declared himself a prophet. He summoned the people to the Mount of Olives where, he proclaimed, he would perform miracles, and enter Jerusalem triumphantly. Felix attacked him, and many of his followers were captured and killed. The man himself, however, managed to escape.[51] Another example of the persecuting zeal of Felix was that of Eleazar, the son of Deinaeus, whom he treacherously arrested with the assurance that, if he would present himself willingly to him, he would not suffer any harm. When Eleazar came, Felix sent him to Rome in chains. This man, according to Josephus,

was for twenty years the head of a group whom the
Jewish historian called "brigands" and "robbers."[52]

Felix was bitterly reproached many times by the high
priest, Jonathan, for his numerous brutal acts and for
the shedding of innocent blood. Jonathan, responsible
for the political appointment of Felix, assumed the
right to criticize and reproach the procurator. Felix
repaid him by hiring assassins to kill him.[53] From 61
C.E. to 66 C.E. three other procurators ruled Judea,
Festus, Albinus and Florus. They continued the policies
of Pontius Pilate and Felix, plundering and crucifying
all those Jews who still possessed sufficient determination to fight for the liberation and independence of
their country.

Conditions degenerated. And in the year 66 C.E., the
great war against Rome broke out.

The political situation was complicated by social and
economic strife among the Jews themselves. Antagonism
sharpened between the high priests and the farmer
folk of Judea from whom the high priests drew their
sustenance in the form of tithes. The farmers looked
upon the priests as hirelings of Rome, and refused to
surrender their tithes for their support. The high
priests, protected by the Roman authorities, seized their
tithes by armed force. This made for estrangement and
bitter resentment between these two classes.

Roman policy always sought to confer protection
upon the wealthy classes, most of whom were the large
landowners. For this protection, the landowners sacrificed national pride, and made every compromise with
their Roman overlords. They placed personal interest

above that of the national welfare. The people regarded them as traitors who were willing, for their own advantage, to recognize Roman authority as supreme.

Intense hatred developed between the masses and the wealthy classes. In the civil strife in Judea, a few short years before the destruction of the Temple, the masses gained momentary power. Men of wealth and of noble families were murdered. The desire for revenge against their old oppressors led to massacres.[54] And, amidst a terrorism comparable only to that which took place later in the French and Russian revolutions, the Jewish state, like a building burning from within and from without, collapsed in the flames of war.

CHAPTER IV

SOCIAL CLASSES AND SOCIAL STRIFE

WITH the establishment of the commonwealth, changes in the economic and social life of the Jewish community took place. These changes had far-reaching consequences. They brought about the emergence of new social groups. They initiated social strife within Judea. They even helped the spread of Christianity later among certain sections of the people. It is a long, intricate and fascinating story, only the barest outline of which can be given here.

Even before the Maccabean period, the social structure of the country had already been modified. The Persian period saw Judea a small, obscure country within the satrapy of Syria. It was so insignificant a country in the vast Persian empire that it was likely called "Philistia" and not Judea. Herodotus, in his History, called the inhabitants of Judea the "Syrians of Palestine."[1] Judea consisted of villages and one important city, Jerusalem. The inhabitants were divided into two classes: one class was composed of the priests and Levites, engaged in the service of the Temple, the other class was made up of the landed folk, the farmers, the so-called *Ame Ha-aretz*.

Priests and Levites received no monetary compensation for their work in the Temple. They and their families had to be maintained. They, therefore, received a tithe from the crops of the farmer folk. They also received gifts from the sacrifices brought to the Temple. The Hebrew names of these tithes were *Terumah,* which the priests received; and *Maasrot* for the Levites. There was an additional *Terumah* which the priests received over and above their regular tithe. So long as the farmers constituted the bulk of the nation and there was no urban life of any importance, they did not withhold the tithe, and willingly sustained the priests and the Levites.

Following the conquest of Judea by the Ptolemies, a new social class emerged which no longer engaged in agriculture, but followed the channels of trade and manufacturing. They received impetus in these directions because of the proximity of the Mediterranean Sea, and the great seaport of Alexandria. Commerce grew by leaps and bounds in Judea. Many Jews who held high positions in the Ptolemian court as tax collectors greatly helped and encouraged the development of this middle class of artisans and traders. With the development of the commonwealth, this group increased its prominence and power. Cities along the coast were annexed to Judea either by penetration or conquest. Galilee to the north—inhabited by Gentiles —was also added to Judea. Trade and commerce flourished. The urban population rapidly expanded. New cities were built. In the course of time the people of Judea which, up to the Hellenistic period, consisted of two classes, added another social class—an urban population.

Hitherto, as pointed out above, the farmer folk, the *Ame Ha-aretz,* and they alone under the Biblical law, supported the priests and the Levites. Now, however, they grew restive and resented the fact that the urban population did not share in the costs of maintenance of the clergy. Many of the farmers, therefore, began to withhold their tithes.[2] Priests, and especially the Levites, did not receive their due allotment of sustenance. Of course, the farmers refused to take into consideration the fact that when they gave their tithes, they increased their prices on their grain to meet their taxes. As a matter of fact, the burden of the tithes was distributed over the consumers as well as over the farmers.

The economic status of the Levites began to deteriorate. To improve the economic conditions of the Levites, the leaders of the Jews ordered the person who purchased from the farmer to give the tithe, disregarding the word of the farmer. The farmer was not to be trusted in reference to the tithe.[3] This injunction, moreover, could not have any deleterious effect on commerce. The leaders further ordained that only those who bought for personal consumption should give a tithe. If, however, the produce was bought from the farmer for commercial purposes, the produce was exempt from the tax. This was done so that the Jews of Judea might be able to compete with the merchants of Syria and Egypt where there was no tithe upon their produce.

The high priests considered the tithe as their personal property. They requisitioned the tithe from the farmers by force, if necessary. Some of the high priests even sent their slaves to seize the tithe, and if the farmers withheld it, they empowered the slaves to beat them with clubs.[4] The Pharisees vigorously condemned such acts of violence.

The city dwellers were called *Haberim*, members of the community. In time, they sought to protect their rights and defend their interests by political institutions. Thus, some of the larger cities in Judea, enjoying internal autonomy, set up their own city council called *Heber-Boule*.[5] Such cities had their own Sanhedrin.

Antagonism sprang up between the farmers, the *Ame Ha-aretz*, and the *Haberim*, the city dwellers. This antagonism spread from the economic to the social realm. The *Haberim* would hardly associate with the *Ame Ha-aretz*. They would not partake of food with them, since the latter were suspected of not having given the required tithe to the Levites; hence, their food could not be used by those Jews who carefully observed the laws of the Pentateuch.[6]

Moreover, the very occupation of the farmer folk of those days made it impossible for them to acquire the graces, the social amenities, the cultural values that lend charm and loveliness to life; these were available to the city folk. The farmers, to extract a mere living from the soil, had to work hard in the fields from early morning until late at night. Theirs was a hard life, made doubly so by their constant warfare against inclement weather, lack of water, excess heat, and destructive insects. They, therefore, did not have the leisure time to cultivate themselves and become educated in the Jewish law, nor to acquire the other amenities of leisured living. The laws of levitical purity—a matter of serious importance—could not be observed by the farmers.

The *Haberim*, the city dwellers, on the other hand, despite their various occupations—trade, commerce, the arts and industries—had more time for themselves, and could more easily educate themselves as well as their children. Consequently, the *Haberim* who conformed to the laws of purity would not associate with the *Ame Ha-aretz*. Needless to say, the farmers resented this attitude bitterly, and tensions that developed into hatred grew up between *Ame Ha-aretz* and *Haberim*. On the other hand, the *Haberim* looked down on the farmer folk as the lower class in Jewish society.[7]

In time, the words *Ame Ha-aretz* which originally meant "farmer folk" came to be synonymous with "ignorance." It became an epithet of contempt and reproach for those who were considered ignorant, crude, immoral, and who did not observe the Jewish law. The word "pagan," from the Latin *paganus,* originally also meant "countryman," but later became the description of people who were irreligious. Similarly, the word "boor" or "hick" (farmer) is now occasionally applied to any rude or ill-bred person. The word *Haber* which signified a man who shared in the city government became the descriptive name of those who were cultured, and knew and observed the Law, especially those who were scrupulously exact concerning the laws of purity. In like manner, the word "urbane," from the Latin *urbanus,* meaning "belonging to the city," has become descriptive of the person whose manners and ways of life are courteous and refined.

The acrimonious feelings between the different social classes in Judea derived from their economic differences and their cultural distinctions. This antagonism was especially manifested against the Galileans, for Galilee was essentially an agricultural province. Josephus pictures Galilee as a land where everyone devoted himself to agriculture. "Every inch of the soil," he wrote, "has been cultivated by the inhabitants."[8] Thus, the Galileans were mostly *Ame Ha-aretz*, farmers, and, suffering the handicaps of farmer folk, were for the most part unlettered and uncultured.

Besides farming, the Galileans also engaged in fishing. The Sea of Galilee was full of different varieties of fish.[9] And numerous fishing smacks plied its waters. So plentiful were the fish that many villages surrounding the lake were inhabited wholly by fishermen. But the leaders in Judea looked upon the Galileans with contempt for being ignorant of the Law. A current proverb in Judea declared, "Out of Galilee ariseth no prophet!"[10] The Gospel according to John states that, when Jesus came to Jerusalem, many said, "This is the Christ"; but some exclaimed, "Shall Christ come out of Galilee?"[11]

Class conflict was inevitable where such tensions and antagonisms flourished. The city folk, the *Haberim*, not only mistrusted the *Ame Ha-aretz*, the farmers, but looked down upon them. The farmers of Judea, as well as those of Galilee, answered this contempt with resentment and scorn. These were the emotional strains that accompanied the economic tensions due to conflicts over tithes and taxes.

Many of the *Ame Ha-aretz*, the farmers, especially those of Galilee, became the rank and file of the various revolutionary sects which stood for such democratic ideals as "equality of men before God." The masses enthusiastically joined such movements which preached the principle of equality. They smarted under the whip of social and cultural degradation, they keenly felt the injustice of social snobbery, and even more sharply they suffered under inequitable economic forces.

From Galilee came forth two men who were kindled with the same ideal of social and economic equality—Judas of Galilee and Jesus of Nazareth. Both Jesus and Judas preached that there is but one ruler over mankind and He is the Lord. They sought out their followers from among the farmer folk of Galilee. And the first disciples of Jesus were humble people—the fishers, the farmers, the toilers of the land in Galilee.

CHAPTER V

THE TWO SANHEDRINS

REVOLUTIONARY changes in government bring about fundamental modifications in the institutions of a people's life. It was inevitable that the whole structure of Jewish social, economic and religious life should be affected by the transformation of the Jewish state from that of a theocracy to that of a commonwealth. From top to bottom Jewish life had to undergo readjustments, especially in its judiciary system. The legal structure of a nation is like the spinal column of an individual; it integrates and supports the whole organism of society. If the organic pattern is changed the legal structure must change with it, if the organism is to continue to function. In the fundamental and far-reaching change within the Jewish social organism—from theocracy to commonwealth—the legal institutions of the state also had to change fundamentally.

Previous to the Maccabean period the high priest held complete civil and religious authority. He was the pontifical head of both religion and state. He derived his religious authority from sanctions within the Pentateuch. And his high position was considered hereditary, being held within the family of Zaddok. His civil authority he received at first from the Persian kings, and later from the Ptolemean and Seleucidean rulers. As high priest, he was empowered to appoint judges to try those who transgressed the religious law, and these judges were responsible only to him.[1] In civil matters, the high priest summoned from time to time representatives of the Jewish aristocracy to a council which was called *Gerousia*, modeled, most likely, after that of the city of Sparta. In affairs concerning the state, he would convene a Great Synagogue as occasion required to guide him in pending decisions.[2]

After the Maccabean revolt, with the emergence of the commonwealth, the position of the high priest was radically transformed. Simon was elected the first ruler with full authority over the Jews. He was also elected to the high priesthood by the Great Synagogue, although he was not of the high priestly family of Zaddok; and the high priesthood was conferred upon him "as an eternal heritage." It is important to note that this honor and authority Simon received by the will of the people and not by any prescribed right. He was given authority, however, only over the Temple and its services. His power did not extend beyond the Temple and its concerns into the wider religious life of the people such as religious law. Thus, for the first time since the Restoration, the high priesthood was stripped of its universal religious authority.

To deal with matters of religious law, an independent institution was created, a court of justice. This court of justice was called in the Hebrew, *Bet Din*; but it is better known to the world by its Greek name, *Sunedrion*—Sanhedrin.

1. THE RELIGIOUS SANHEDRIN

The Religious Sanhedrin was made up of different branches. One was composed of seventy-one (or seventy-two) judges, and was a legislative body whose function was to interpret the Biblical law and fix the *Halakah* (the law). This Sanhedrin held its sessions in the Hall of Hewn Stone (a compartment in the Temple).[3] At the head of the Sanhedrin presided the *Nasi*, the president of the court, and the *Ab Bet Din*, the vice-president. In the early period of the institution, the heads of the Sanhedrin were of the priestly family; in later times nonpriestly Israelites sat over the Sanhedrin. The first Israelite to preside over the Sanhedrin was Shemaiah and was succeeded by Hillel, whose office became hereditary in his family. The family, according to a later tradition, was descended from the royal family of David.[4]

The Sanhedrin held religious authority not only over Judea, but over the entire Jewry of the then-known world. The spiritual needs of all the Jews and their laws were directed by the Sanhedrin. It alone had power to fix the calendar, to intercalate the necessary months in a leap year, to establish the holydays in their proper season, and to legislate laws concerning marriage and divorce.[5]

The Sanhedrin of seventy-one never tried cases which involved capital punishment, since it was only a legislative body. In certain cases, however, the Sanhedrin acted as a trial court, such cases as the trial of the head of the state, the high priest, for offense against the state or the Temple. The Sanhedrin of seventy-one also sat as a trial court in a case against a city whose inhabitants were led astray to worship foreign gods, or against an entire tribe that revolted against the state. A false prophet, namely a person who asserted that his prophecies derived from foreign gods, could also be tried by the Sanhedrin of seventy-one.[6]

But these were merely theoretical, constitutional rights of the Sanhedrin which had never actually been exercised. The Jews were not divided into tribes during the Second Commonwealth, nor was there any case of a city declared condemned because its inhabitants went astray after foreign gods; there were no prophets of idolatry in that period. Monotheism had become so deeply rooted among the Jews that polytheism was a dead issue. Nor had the Sanhedrin ever tried a king or a high priest. In the early days of the commonwealth, the high priests were of the Hasmonean family who also ruled as kings. The Sanhedrin had no power over them; and in later years, the high priests were appointed by King Herod or by the Roman government, and the Sanhedrin certainly could not exercise jurisdiction over them.

A Sanhedrin composed of twenty-three members tried cases involving religious offenses such as homicide, incest, and profanation of the Sabbath publicly for which punishment incurring death was meted out. There was one such Sanhedrin in every important city of Judea. In Jerusalem there were three such Sanhedrins; one in the city proper, another on the Temple Mount, and one in the Temple Court. These Sanhedrins of twenty-three were called "the small Sanhedrin" to distinguish them from the Sanhedrin of seventy-one.[7]

The Sanhedrin which tried capital punishment cases held their sessions every day of the week, except Saturdays and holydays, and on the days preceding them.

They never conducted sessions at night. A person who stood trial could be acquitted by the court on the same day, but the law forbade that a conviction should take place on the day the trial began. A verdict of guilt must be postponed until the following day. Consequently, courts did not hold sessions on the eves of Saturday and holydays.[8] The court could not possess knowledge in advance of the decision that would be reached, whether it would be acquittal or conviction of the offender. If the court should convict the offender, they would have to give the verdict on the morrow. However, the morrow was a Saturday or holyday and not a court day. Thus, they would have to postpone the verdict to the following day, i.e., after the Saturday or the holyday. This was contradictory to the Jewish conception of justice. That was the reason why no courts were held on the eves of Saturdays and holydays.

Josephus[9] records an interesting case illustrative of the Jewish law that conviction could not take place on the day of the opening of the trial. It concerned Herod, when, as a young man, he was governor of Galilee. He had ordered the killing of Hezekiah, the father of Judas, and other young men on the pretext that they were robbers. Their mothers and relatives demanded that King John Hyrcanus II bring Herod to trial for his murderous acts. Since Herod had not executed these men by royal command, he was considered a commoner in the eyes of the law, and therefore had to appear before the Sanhedrin of twenty-three.

The king summoned Herod to Jerusalem. Herod came, dressed in military attire, and carried with him, as protection, a letter from Sextius Caesar, the Roman governor of Syria, to King Hyrcanus. In this letter Sextius Caesar urged King Hyrcanus to see that no harm should befall Herod. According to the Jewish law, Herod could not have been convicted of manslaughter, for he had not actually himself killed the men. He had ordered his soldiers to do so. He was in the category of instigator, and his crime according to the *Halakah*, was not punishable by death. Only the actual slayer was subject to capital punishment.[10]

A member of the Sanhedrin, however, named Sameas (Shemaiah), had a presentiment that Herod would some day become king. He appealed, therefore, to the Sanhedrin to avail itself of the opportunity to convict Herod and put him out of the way. He warned the members of the Sanhedrin that, if they lost this opportunity, Herod, when he became king, would kill all the members of the Sanhedrin including the regnant king, though he was his patron and protector. Sameas, in order to convict Herod of a capital offense, interpreted a Biblical passage to mean that an instigator to a crime should be accounted equally guilty with the perpetrator himself and should be made to suffer the same penalty.[11]

His speech and foresightedness had great influence over the members of the Sanhedrin and they were ready to convict Herod. But Hyrcanus, who was anxious to save Herod, made use of the law by which a man could not be convicted on the day on which his trial began. Accordingly, he adjourned the court, and advised Herod to leave the city. Incidentally, the law which Sameas propounded—an instigator is as guilty of crime as the man who actually committed it—never became part of the Jewish law.

This procedure—that the Sanhedrin was never in session on Saturdays, holydays and the eves of those days—was recognized by the Roman authorities, even outside of Judea. Augustus Caesar once wrote to the Praetor that the Jews should not be compelled to appear for trial before a judge on *paresque*—the day of preparation—Friday after the ninth hour (3 P.M.).[12]

While the Sanhedrin of twenty-three had the authority to inflict either corporal punishment or death upon the offenders, the Bible permits the employment of only four modes of capital punishment: stoning, burning, decapitation, and strangling.[13]

The constitution of the Sanhedrin protected the rights of the defendant. If the defendant thought that the decision was rendered against him due to misinterpretation of the law by the judges, he had the right to take a *cassatio* to a higher court. He and the *mufla* —rhetor—(the prosecuting attorney) of the lower court went to the court which held its session on the Temple Mount. The *mufla* was the man who argued the case against the defendant. He was called the *mufla*, the speaker, in the court. If the defendant, however, was still not satisfied with the decision of this court, he had the right to make his *cassatio* to the court which held its sessions in the Temple Court. Finally he could take his *cassatio* to the Sanhedrin of seventy-one, not for retrial but for examination of the decision which had been rendered by the lower court.[14]

The members of the Sanhedrin were Pharisees. The decisions of the courts were rendered according to the Pharisaic doctrines. If Sadducees sometimes became judges, they had to render the decisions according to the Pharisaic interpretations. Josephus states that when Sadducees were appointed to the courts they adjusted themselves to the notions of the Pharisees, because the multitude would not otherwise tolerate them.[15] Likewise, from the *Tannaitic* literature, we know quite well that the Sadducees had to follow the laws as they were interpreted and rendered by the Pharisees.[16]

The religious Sanhedrin lasted in Judea until the destruction of the Temple.[17] The Sanhedrin of twenty-three had full power to condemn a Jew for transgressing the religious law even to the extent of inflicting capital punishment. From the *Tannaitic* literature, we know of a case where, but a few years before the destruction of the Temple, the Sanhedrin convicted the daughter of a priest for committing adultery. She was put to death.[18] Josephus, likewise, tells us that Titus, at the siege of Jerusalem, appealed to the Jews to surrender, and argued that the Romans never interfered in the religious life of the Jews, even when they put to death a Roman citizen for passing beyond the barriers of the sanctuary.[19] According to the Jewish law, no foreigner was permitted to enter the Temple Court. This was respected by the Roman authorities. It was considered a capital offense for any pagan to pass beyond the barriers of the sanctuary. Indeed, slabs were placed in front of the Temple with inscriptions in Greek and Latin prohibiting a non-Jew from entering the holy place under penalty of death.[20]

Both Philo[21] and Josephus[22] testify that the Romans never changed any Jewish customs or religious laws. The procurators generally abstained from all interference with the customs of the country. The policy of imperial Rome was always that of tolerance for all existing religions. In fact, the religions of the subjugated peoples were protected.[23] The Jewish religion had enjoyed that protection since the time of Julius Caesar. There were only two cases in which the Romans disregarded the Jewish religion. Once, when Pontius Pilate brought his Roman legion into Jerusalem with the figure of the emperor on its flags, and the second case, when Emperor Gaius Caligula ordered that his statue should be set up in the Temple. Excepting these two cases, the Roman authorities never interfered with the Jewish religion, even when Judea became a Roman province.

2. THE POLITICAL SANHEDRIN

Besides the religious Sanhedrin, there was another Sanhedrin whose main function was to try offenders against the state. This Sanhedrin might well be designated the political Sanhedrin. It differed from the religious Sanhedrin both in character and constitution.

The establishment of the political Sanhedrin was necessitated by the political changes which occurred in Judea. In the time of the theocracy as was pointed out before, one man, the high priest, controlled the entire life of the nation. Any person who committed an of

fense against God or the state was tried by a court
under his supervision. With the establishment of the
commonwealth, and later the monarchy, the ruler or
the king had no power to interfere with the religious
life of the Jews. The religious Sanhedrin was entirely
independent of the civil authority. According to its constitution, it had no jurisdiction over political offenders.
It tried only those who transgressed against the laws
of the Bible. A new court had to be established to deal
with those who transgressed against the laws of the
state or against the ruler himself.

The religious Sanhedrin was guided by statutes. Before convicting a man, this court was very careful in
the examination of witnesses. The defendant, if dissatisfied, had recourse to the right of appeal. It held its
sessions in specified places, every day except Saturdays,
holydays and eves of those days. It never convicted a
man on the day that his trial began. Its members were
scholars appointed first to the lower courts and then
elevated to the higher court, because of their achieve-
ment in scholarship.

The political Sanhedrin, on the other hand, did not
have to have scholars as its members. The state, through
its rulers, appointed the members of the court. And the
head of the state, it may be presumed, appointed such
men as members whom he believed would render
verdicts according to his wishes. Hence, the members of
this Sanhedrin were merely puppets carrying out the
wishes of their ruler. Since the political Sanhedrin was
not guided by statutes, it had no definite place to meet,

and it tried its cases any time, day or night, Saturdays, holydays, or weekdays.

There were essential differences between these two types of Sanhedrin. When a man transgressed against a law of a religious character, he was summoned *vocure in jus* before the religious Sanhedrin which held its sessions in designated places and at specific times. Josephus tells us that Herod was summoned to appear before the court when he was accused of killing innocent men in Galilee. He was then a commoner so he had to answer the charge of murder before the religious Sanhedrin.[24] The *Tannaitic* literature, likewise speaking about the session of this Sanhedrin, always used the term "sitting." And in reference to the ordering of the litigants to appear, it used the term "summoned."

If a man, however, was accused of committing a crime against the state, or offended the ruler, he was arrested and a Sanhedrin was called into special sitting by the ruler. In reality, the political Sanhedrin did not go through the motions of justice, it was a mock trial, since it had to carry out the whim of the master and ruler. Furthermore, if a man was put to death by the religious Sanhedrin, the law provided that his property passed to his heirs. In the case of execution by decree of the political Sanhedrin, the state confiscated the victim's property.[25] Even the clothing which he wore at the time of execution was seized by the state.

Of the religious Sanhedrin we have a detailed account in the *Tannaitic* literature, of the political Sanhedrin we find evidence in Josephus. Josephus recorded a number of cases in which the political Sanhedrin was summoned to fulfill the arbitrary whims of the ruler. Some of them follow:

According to Josephus, King Herod was not confident of the security of his throne as long as the deposed King Hyrcanus was alive. He, therefore, plotted to kill him. To do this, he called a Sanhedrin, and produced a letter which Hyrcanus supposedly wrote to Malchus, governor of Arabia, accusing the deposed king of *lèse-majesté*.[26] That this Sanhedrin was a political Sanhedrin can be inferred from the fact that there is no law in the Bible, or in the *Tannaitic* literature, which would condemn an intriguer against the king to death. The fact that Herod summoned a Sanhedrin to try Hyrcanus proves that it was a political Sanhedrin; otherwise, Herod would have summoned Hyrcanus to appear before the religious Sanhedrin as was the practice among the Jews.

On another occasion, Herod, in order to kill his wife, Mariamne, convened a Sanhedrin and accused her of adultery.[27] He had no witnesses to testify that she had committed this crime. According to the Biblical law, as well as the *Tannaitic* law, she could not be punished by death.

Again, King Herod, apprehensive lest his sons, the children of Mariamne, have designs on his kingdom, called a Sanhedrin before which he charged them with disloyalty to himself and to the state.[28] They were later put to death. Undoubtedly, this, too, was the work of the political Sanhedrin.

Another time Herod assembled a Sanhedrin and

brought charges against his sister-in-law, the wife of his brother, Pheroras, for bewitching the latter with drugs to alienate him from Herod.[29] There is no law in the Bible, or in the *Tannaitic* literature, which provides that a court can punish a person for alienation of affections. Here, too, it was the political Sanhedrin which had been summoned by Herod.

It is true that Herod as a tyrant put many men to death without any trial, but sometimes even a dictator, for the sake of public opinion, is forced to conduct a mock trial.

From Josephus we learn that the Levites insisted that King Agrippa permit them to wear linen garments such as were worn by the priests. To act on their demands, King Agrippa called a Sanhedrin which granted the Levites their request.[30] This Sanhedrin could only have been political. The demands of the Levites to wear linen garments in the Temple were motivated by social reasons not by religious ones. They wanted to raise their status equal to that of the priests. The priests wore linen garments at their functions in the Temple, so the Levites wanted also to wear linen garments when they sang their hymns to God in the Temple.

It is noteworthy that in all these cases the defendants were first arrested, and then a Sanhedrin was *summoned*. As pointed out above, there was no occasion for the religious Sanhedrin to be summoned since it held its sessions daily, except on Saturdays and on holydays. Hence, besides the actual nature of the cases treated, the punishments meted out, and the kind of laws that were enforced, the calling of the Sanhedrin indicates clearly that a political Sanhedrin existed as the willing tool of the ruler's whims and desires.

We have reason to assume that these two types of Sanhedrin came into being at the same time when the commonwealth was established. The span of life of the political Sanhedrin, however, was much shorter than that of the religious Sanhedrin. When the Romans conquered Judea and made it a Roman province, the political Sanhedrin ceased as a Jewish institution.

Prior to the conquest of Judea, if the ruler had a case against any individual, he summoned the political Sanhedrin to pass judgment upon him; then the ruler carried out the punishment of the culprit. With the conquest of the country by the Romans, the procurator assumed entire authority of the legal procedure. He passed judgment and inflicted punishment on the accused charged with seditious acts against the state. The high priests were appointed by the procurator. They were men whom the authorities knew would execute their policies. To them the procurator entrusted the task of enforcing political and social order in Judea. The high priests were responsible to the Romans for the tranquillity of their country. It was their duty to hunt out the malcontents, the rebels against the state, and to report them to the Roman officials. Dependent on the Roman procurator, they proved obedient servants to their masters. Watchdogs of the Roman imperialism, some of them were even ready to exterminate Jews who raised arms against their conquerors.

The high priests were reduced to agents of the procurator. They arrested those considered a menace to the state, summoned a Sanhedrin before which they presented the evidence in the case for the procurator; then the procurator passed judgment on the convicted and carried out the punishment. Thus, we may describe some of the high priests in the time of Jesus as being like the "Quislings" of our own troublesome days.

Josephus tells us that in the interval between the death of the Procurator Festus (in the year 62 C.E.) and the arrival of his successor, Albinus, a Sanhedrin was convened by Ananus, the high priest. This Sanhedrin condemned and put to death James, the brother of Jesus, for transgressing the law.[31] Some Jews who were dissatisfied with the high priest, Ananus, accused him before King Agrippa II and Procurator Albinus of having acted illegally in summoning a Sanhedrin to try James and put him to death.

Josephus does not tell us for what kind of crime James was condemned to death. Was his crime religious or political? The fact that the high priest, Ananus, convened a Sanhedrin to try James gives us reason to believe that the high priest considered James a political offender. He was the brother of Jesus. He was accused most likely by the high priest as a follower of the new sect, *the Nazarenes*—Christians. The calling of the Sanhedrin and the carrying out of the punishment against James were done by Ananus on his own responsibility. He had been appointed by King Agrippa II. Since the death of his father, Agrippa I, the appointment of the high priest had been taken from the pro-

curator by Claudius Caesar and entrusted to his son,
Agrippa II. For his actions, however, the high priest
was responsible to the Roman procurator. Hence, he
had no right to call a Sanhedrin without first consult-
ing King Agrippa and, certainly, he had no power to
put anyone to death for political reasons. The rights
of capital punishment for a political offense rested in
the hands of the procurator. Thus, the countercharges
which the Jews brought against Ananus were that he
had assembled a Sanhedrin without the knowledge
of King Agrippa, and that he had put James to death
in the absence of the Roman procurator, having no
authority to do so. Albinus threatened to punish
Ananus. King Agrippa promptly dismissed him from
the high priesthood.

During the revolt against the Romans, the Jews
gained their independence momentarily. Again the political Sanhedrin became a Jewish institution. Josephus
relates that the Zealots, in order to put to death an
influential man by the name Zacharias, the son of
Baris, convened a Sanhedrin.[32] Zacharias was accused
by the Zealots of holding treasonable communications
with the Romans. He was tried by the Sanhedrin for
betraying the Jewish state to the enemies of Judea.
He was condemned and put to death. His property
was confiscated by the Zealots. According to the law of
the country, anyone who was put to death for a political offense had his property taken over by the state.

Thus, we have established the existence at the time
of Jesus of two types of Sanhedrin, a religious Sanhedrin
about which we learn from the *Tannaitic* literature, and
the political Sanhedrin, which Josephus records.

CHAPTER VI

PARTIES, SECTS AND PHILOSOPHIES

IN THE stormy Judea of the crucial first century of the Christian Era, when Sadducee and Pharisee, king and high priest, farmer and townsman, Roman and Jew were locked in desperate struggle, the Jewish people's instinct to survive sought expression in sects and philosophies, as well as in political parties that led their adherents into strange, devious, and even dark and violent ways. It is now an accepted fact of historical interpretation that political and even some religious philosophies of national life emerge out of the social and economic struggles within the nation. These conflicting philosophies provide the rationale by which men interpret to themselves and to others the objectives they seek to achieve, and justify the enormous sacrifices they must make in the realization of their purposes. In a profoundly true sense "ideas are weapons" in the struggle for existence.

In a people religiously nurtured as were the Jews, theological and religious concepts provided the forms and instrumentalities for vital forces of challenge to the existing social order, and for change and revolt. The heavy oppression of Rome, worked through her greedy and shortsighted procurators, and the sharp social and economic tensions within Jewish life inevitably gave birth to different political parties, philosophical faiths and religious sects. In the time of Jesus, these growing forces came to their maturity and met in open and violent conflict.

1. PHARISEES AND SADDUCEES—THEIR BELIEFS

Of the origin as well as the names, "Sadducees" and "Pharisees," and with some of their political and social doctrines, we have already dealt.[1] But they held characteristic theological ideas as well, and they exerted powerful influence in different social groups in the population. Josephus, who is the primary source of our information about the different sects which existed during the Second Commonwealth, brings his testimony about the beliefs of the Sadducees and Pharisees—beliefs corroborated in the *Talmud* and the New Testament. Josephus was well placed to know all the forces and influences of his times, because he was born just a few years after the crucifixion of Jesus, and, in order to learn about the various sects and parties, had joined all of them at various times.

About the Sadducees, Josephus wrote that they denied predestination and divine influence on man's acts, whether they be good or bad. Everything, according to them, lies in man's hands, and man alone is responsible for his happy or adverse lot in life. They believed only in the *Torah*, the Written Law; and they denied the validity and binding power of the Tradition of the sages, the Oral Law.[2] Unlike other religious sects, the Sadducees denied the existence of angels.[3] They were of the opinion that the soul dies with the body. Justice and punishment, they held, must be administered in this world since they did not believe in reward and punishment in the world beyond the grave.[4] Josephus describes the Sadducees as rude in their behavior among themselves, and with people outside their group. They were harsh in their judgments. They had no followers among the populace, though some officials and wealthy Jews were influenced by their teachings.[5] We have already learned that they denied that God made a covenant with David that the kingdom should belong to his children.

The beliefs of the Pharisees ran diametrically opposite to those of the Sadducees. As already stated, the Pharisees laid great importance upon the Oral Law. They held that Divine Providence governed all the acts of a man, though they also believed that free choice was man's also, for his is the power to choose the good or the evil. They believed in reward and punishment in the future world, and in resurrection. They regarded the soul as immortal.[6] They held men of age and of wisdom in high respect, and obeyed the laws with precise exactness. The Pharisees exerted great and wide influence over the masses of the people. All the more so, because they were lenient in their judgments, and never applied to those who ran athwart the law any severe punishment.[7] So extensive was their influence over the people that, if a Sadducee was ever appointed a judge, he had to follow the laws prescribed by the Pharisees, since otherwise the people would not put up with him.[8]

The teachings of the Pharisees were followed by the people from the time of the establishment of the commonwealth to the destruction of the Temple, save in

the time of Janneus Alexander and during the civil
wars. The people were devoted to the Pharisees for
their piety and virtues. In the Gospels, however, they
are portrayed as "hypocrites." Why this was so presents
a problem which will be discussed later, but one must
point out here that to call the Pharisees as a group
"hypocrites" was unjust. Undoubtedly, as in any other
group, individuals are always found who justly merit
harsh judgment from their betters; but, surely, distinction must be made between the true and the false followers of any way of life. Unscrupulous people often
join a popular movement merely to further their own
interests. Association with a distinguished group casts
its aura of respectability over questionable characters,
at least until exposure reveals the culprits. Meanwhile
such men may bring shame and even disaster to a
worthy social movement. Certainly in the case of the
Pharisees evil and designing men joined them in ordei
to gain their own ends. The Talmud took cognizance
of them. In the story that depicts the deathbed scene
of Janneus Alexander, the dying man warned his wife
that she should not fear the genuine Pharisees or the
Sadducees, but that she should beware of those unscrupulous persons who, in the guise of Pharisees, continued in their evil course and worked wicked deeds.[9]

Among the Pharisees, the elderly and scholarly element, despairing at the many misfortunes that had be-
fallen the commonwealth—monarchy, civil wars, Roman domination—had turned away from preoccupation
with worldly matters, and chosen, rather, the quiet and
shaded groves of contemplative religion. After Herod

usurped the kingdom of Judea, these Pharisees became
Quietists. They turned to religion, which they held
could never be disturbed by earthly powers, the spirit
being transcendent over the sword. Furthermore, this
scholarly element of the Pharisees, given to exact and
scrupulous observance of the law, became known as
"legalists." The younger group, however, continued
their interest in worldly affairs. They preached and
fought for the independence of the Jewish state. They
proclaimed their adherence to the Pharisaic doctrine
that a Jewish Kingdom would be re-established under
the anointed Messiah of the family of the house of
David. Their national aspirations were rooted in the
faith that God would assemble all the Jews from the
corners of the earth and set up over them the scepter
of a scion of David.

2. THE ESSENES

Besides the Pharisees and the Sadducees, we learn
from Philo[10] and Josephus,[11] there was a third group
or sect called the "Essenes." The Essenes are mentioned by name only in Philo and Josephus; the Talmud has not recorded the name of this sect, hence we
do not know its Hebrew form. Nor are the Essenes
mentioned in the New Testament. Since many New
Testament scholars believe that the Essenes had some
influence on the origin of Christianity,[12] it is necessary
to give a short account of the philosophy of this sect.

The name "Essenes," according to the most widely
accepted opinion, is derived from the Hebrew name
Hasidim, "the Pietists."[13] The *Hasidim*, we pointed

out above, were zealous in the observance of God's commands and were concerned mainly with the character and destiny of their own souls. They were keen individualists, and, as such, were never concerned with the Jews as a people. To be sure, they allied themselves with the Hasmoneans at one time, but only when the Jewish religion was on the verge of destruction by the Syrians. As soon as the Jews won their religious freedom, the *Hasidim* withdrew from their alliance. They were not interested in helping the Hasmoneans to establish an independent Jewish state.

The Essenes appear to have been the successors of the early *Hasidim*. Like them, the Essenes were highly individualistic in their attitudes toward Jewish life. Many of the Essenes' beliefs may be traced to influences derived from the *Hasidim*. For example, the *Hasidim* protested against the appointment of Jonathan and, later, Simon as high priests, because they were not of the family of Zaddok; they considered this a profanation of the Temple. The Essenes, because of that incident, refused to send any sacrifice to the Temple. They appointed priests of their own, and for the Temple altar substituted their own table. Moreover, they were opposed to anointing with oil, on the ground that such anointing was reserved for high priests and kings of the Davidic family. Before every meal they bathed their bodies in cold water, and before partaking of food a priest said grace.[14]

They were strict in the observance of the laws of the Bible, and since they could not observe the laws in the cities where the Pharisees had modified the *Halakot* (the laws), they formed communities of their own. In these communities they found it possible to live in accordance with their own customs.

Due to the fact that the Essenes did not participate in the social and economic and political life of the Jewish people, and lived apart in their own communities, they became in time a semimonastic order. They held all property in common. Some of them rejected the institution of marriage, while others cohabited with their wives only for the sake of having children. They would adopt the children of other parents to insure the continuation of their group life. They dressed in white garments, perhaps as symbols of purity and cleanliness.

Josephus wrote that the Essenes displayed extraordinary interest in the writings of the ancients, "singling out in particular those which make for the welfare of soul and body. With the help of these and with a view to the treatment of diseases, they make investigations into medicinal cures." They attached great importance to the art of predicting the future, and, according to Josephus, they seldom, if ever, erred in their prophecies. They believed that the body was corruptible, but the soul was imperishable and immortal. For good deeds done in this world, they believed that men would be rewarded after death.

The Essenes held that all things were predestined and determined. They believed in the absolute rule of Fate, and denied that men had free will. They held all rulers in high esteem and obeyed them, because, believing in Fate, they believed that no man could attain to any office save by the will of God.[15] Their rule of life was love. For them love of God, love of virtue, and love of their fellow man, was the motto by which they lived. It is quite likely that John the Baptist was either a member of the Essenes, or else was greatly influenced by the beliefs of this semimonastic order.

3. THE FOURTH PHILOSOPHY—THE SICARII

Josephus, in describing the various sects and parties, writes about two other groups that were active in Judea. These groups were, in reality, offshoots of the Pharisees. One, Josephus named the "Fourth Philosophy,"[16] because this group came fourth after the Pharisees, the Sadducees and the Essenes. There was still another group which Josephus permits to remain nameless, but which, for reasons to be given later, might well be called the "Apocalyptic-Pharisees."

Josephus gives a detailed account of the Fourth Philosophy. From his description, the true character of the tenets of this sect, as well as their violent deeds, can be learned.

Undoubtedly, the first appearance of the Fourth Philosophy was made when Augustus Caesar annexed Judea, and declared it a province of Rome in the year 6 C.E. At that time Quirinius was sent to take a census of Judea, with a view to levying taxes upon the people. Against the imposition and collection of these taxes Judas of Galilee inveighed, and he incited the Jews to revolt against the Romans, and urged them not to pay taxes. He warned them that in paying taxes they revealed themselves as cowards. More than that, they grovelingly accepted the Romans as their masters while, in reality, according to their faith, there was but one Master whose rule they acknowledged, and that Master was God.[17]

The followers of Judas from time to time committed seditious acts against the Romans. Being a small minority, they were easily suppressed by the Romans and by the puppet government of Judea. Many of them were captured and sent in chains to Rome; others were slain in the mountains. Two sons of Judas, taken captive by Alexander Tiberus, were crucified. Eleazar, the son of Deinaeus, a leader of one of these groups, was imprisoned by Felix and was sent, a captive in chains, to Rome.

The members of this Fourth Philosophy, however, though sorely oppressed, were not entirely destroyed; they continued to fight against the Romans, and were especially hostile against those Jews who were puppets in the hands of the authorities. They plundered the property of those who submitted to the conqueror, and even killed those of their compatriots who joined the Romans. They maintained that such Jews were in no wise different from the Romans, for they betrayed the freedom of the Jewish people in a cowardly manner, a freedom that was worthy of being defended to the death.

Not being able to engage in open battle against the Romans and traitorous Jews, these adherents of the Fourth Philosophy resorted to the use of the *sica* (a short dagger) to get rid of those who favored peace at any price with the enemy. From their use of the *sica*, they received the name the "Sicarii."[18] Josephus refers to this group as *lestai* which in Greek means "robbers," "brigands." And, he makes these *lestai*, "robbers," responsible for all the misfortunes which befell the Jews from the time of Judas of Galilee until the burning of the Temple.

Of course, the verdict of Josephus is a gross distortion of the realities. For Josephus himself describes the hunger for freedom and liberty that motivated these valiant patriots.

They have an inviolable attachment to liberty, and say that God is to be their only Ruler and Lord. They also do not value dying any kind of death, nor indeed do they heed the deaths of their relations and friends, nor can any such fear make them call any man, Lord.[19]

Surely ordinary robbers could not evince such devotion to liberty, a devotion that made them fearless to the extreme. And the speech which, according to Josephus, Eleazar, son of Jairus—the last leader of the Fourth Philosophy—delivered to his followers sounds a clarion call to lovers of freedom. It is a speech that Josephus, in recording, unconsciously offers as convincing evidence against his own opinion of these men.

Long since, my brave men, we determined neither to serve the Romans nor any other save God, for He alone is man's true and righteous Lord; and now the time is come which bids us verify that resolution by our actions. At this crisis let us not disgrace ourselves; we who in the past refused to submit even to a slavery involving no peril, let us not now, along with slavery, deliberately accept the irreparable penalties awaiting us if we are to fall alive into Roman hands. For as we were the first of all to revolt, so are we the last in arms against them. Moreover, I believe that it is God who has granted us this favor, that we have it in our power to die nobly and in freedom—a privilege denied to others who have met with unexpected defeat . . . For it is death which gives liberty to the soul and permits it to depart to its own pure abode, there to be free from all calamity; but so long as it is imprisoned in a mortal body tainted with all its miseries, it is, in sober truth, dead, for association with what is mortal ill befits that which is divine.[20]

Such noble sentiments could not have been uttered, as Josephus would have us believe, by an ordinary robber.

Eleazar delivered this speech in the fortress of Masada. The only survivors in the fortress of Masada were two old women and five children.[21] They did not report this speech to Josephus who was far away from Masada, already enjoying the hospitality of the Flavian family, the conquerors of Judea. It is well known that Josephus, like the Greek historians, composed speeches and put them into the mouths of his heroes. These speeches helped to reveal the character of the speakers far better than lengthy analysis or detailed description. And Josephus, despite his detestation of the *Sicarii*, could not have written this speech and assumed Eleazar a man of such exalted conceptions, if he actually believed him to be, as he called him, "a murderer." This sublime speech of the leader of the *Sicarii* brings to mind the stirring words of one of the greatest leaders of the American Revolution, Patrick Henry, whose immortal words ended with the ringing cry, "Give me liberty, or give me death." Seventeen centuries before Patrick Henry, the *Sicarii* held the same dangerous philosophy of life, that life without liberty was not worth the living. For liberty they would willingly have made every sacrifice, even their very lives.

Again it must be emphasized that designing people often insinuate themselves into the ranks of a revolutionary movement to serve their own ends and purposes, and utilize the party as sanction for their own nefarious deeds. It may well be that some such unscrupulous men impersonated the *Sicarii*, and later were confused with them in the minds of the Jews even at that time. Certainly later, Josephus added to the confusion by his partisan attitude toward the *Sicarii*.[22] This confusion was further confounded by the modern writers. One thought must be held clear about these wielders of the *sica*—they fought for the liberty of their country. And they met death unflinchingly for their devotion to liberty. The Roman authorities, abetted by some Jewish leaders, the Quislings of the first century, crucified them by the thousands.

Often to save their leaders, the *Sicarii* even resorted to kidnaping. Once, they kidnaped an important personage connected with the high priest, and held him as hostage for their leaders whom the procurators had imprisoned.[23] In view of what is happening in our own day, when the Chetniks of Serbia, in order to gain release for their leaders captured by the Germans, kidnaped and held in hostage members of the puppet government of Serbia, we can better appreciate and understand the devices and strategems of the *Sicarii* whose zealous patriotism knew but one goal—freedom.

The *Sicarii*, so named by Josephus, but really members of the Fourth Philosophy, were the true descendants of the Pharisees who fought for freedom in the times of the Hasmoneans. Their forefathers won their freedom; they, through historic circumstances, lost theirs; but both were moved by the same principles and same ideals. They fought and died for the freedom of Judea. They readily sacrificed their lives for their belief in the equality of men. They battled in protest against the lordship of man over man. They met death declaring that only God was the true Lord.

4. THE APOCALYPTIC-PHARISEES

Josephus makes mention of another group active in Judea, but gives it no name; however, he refers to its members as "wicked." Although their hands were purer than those of the *Sicarii*, he wrote, their intentions were the same as those of the *Sicarii* "brigands." This group, according to Josephus, consisted of deceivers and impostors who, under the pretense of divine inspiration, fostered revolution. He continued to say that these men, from time to time, persuaded the people to follow them into the desert with the promise that God would give them a sign of deliverance.[24]

Josephus singled two men out from among the impostors. One was Theudas and the other an Egyptian false prophet. About the former Josephus gives the following account: Theudas promised the people that he would divide the River Jordan for them so they could pass through its waters. Many deluded Jews followed him. Thereupon the procurator, Fadus, seized a number of the Jews, and had Theudas himself executed.[25] Of the false Egyptian prophet, Josephus writes that he invited the people to accompany him to the Mount of Olives. He promised them that by a miracle the walls of Jerusalem would fall down, and the people would march into the city without Roman opposition. The procurator at that time, Felix, had many of these Jews killed.[26] Both these impostors are mentioned in the New Testament.[27]

Josephus includes these impostors with the *Sicarii*. Again, it would be a gross distortion of historical fact to accept Josephus' judgment uncritically. Not all of these men were deceivers. Judea was passing through troublous times, suffering under the humiliating yoke of Rome. And undoubtedly, charlatans and impostors spread their net for the unwary. But there must have been few charlatans who took advantage of these pious Jews. The large number of Jews looked for the day of deliverance when God would free them from Roman servitude, and establish the Kingdom of Heaven.

This group, to which Josephus applies the epithet "sorcerers and deceivers,"[28] was really composed of the Apocalyptic-Pharisees. They believed in the revelation of God, and, therefore, the name "Apocalyptists" is given to them. These Apocalyptic-Pharisees, like the *Sicarii*, preached the gospel: no lordship of man over man; the equality of men; the only ruler over man is God. But, they differed from the *Sicarii* in their method, for the *Sicarii* believed that terror must oppose terror,

and for the establishment of a society of free people,
force and violence, even murder, are justified to destroy
the enemy. The Apocalyptists were opposed to terroristic acts, and the use of violence. They preached love
not violence. "If anyone seeketh to do evil unto you,
do well unto him, and pray for him."[29] That was their
watchword and guide. The Apocalyptic-Pharisees were
God-fearing people, anticipating the day when God
would redeem His own. That such impostors as Theudas
and the false prophet from Egypt were to be found
among them, was not surprising; it is part of human
experience for the false to disguise itself in the habili-
ments of seeming Truth. Indeed, it was to such pretenders that the Gospel according to Matthew alluded
when it said, "For there shall arise false Christs (Mes-
siahs) and false prophets."[30]

Josephus entertained only scorn for the *Sicarii* and
the Apocalyptic-Pharisees. Both of them, to be sure,
stood for revolutionary changes in society and the freedom of the Jews from the Roman yoke, but they differed fundamentally in their methods of achieving their
goals. The *Sicarii* believed in the resort to arms; the
Apocalyptists looked to divine intervention for the
freedom of Israel. Josephus alluded to this latter group
when he wrote:

For there was a certain sect of men that were Jews who
valued themselves highly upon the exact skill they had
in the law of their fathers and made men believe that
they were highly favored by God . . . These are those that
are called the sect of the Pharisees who were in the capacity
of greatly opposing kings.[31]

This group of men were not the Pharisees, the "legal-ists," but the Apocalyptists for whom Josephus had only scorn.[32]

Fortunately, the Apocalyptic-Pharisees have left a considerable literature. *The Book of Enoch,* the *Testament of the Twelve Patriarchs,* and the *Psalms of Solomon* were written by them. Compiled before the Christian Era, they have been preserved to our time, and in their pages we may see the clear picture of the philosophy and beliefs of this Pharisaic sect.

The Apocalyptic-Pharisees held the same beliefs as the Pharisees, "the Quietists." They shared their ideas concerning reward and punishment, Providence, angels, and the coming of the son of David, the Messiah. They laid more stress on these principles than the Pharisees themselves. The Pharisees believed that God would free Israel, and a king of the scion of David would rule over them. This king Messiah would not be a supernatural being, but like Judas Maccabeus or David himself, would be a great general and leader who would avenge Israel, and would free the Jews from their foreign yoke. On the other hand, the Apocalyptic-Pharisees believed that the Jewish Messiah would be a supernatural being, yet a scion of the family of David.[33] In their literature, they called the son of David,[34] "the anointed of God,"[35] "the Elect One,"[36] "the Son of Man,"[37] "the Son of God."[38]

The Apocalyptic-Pharisees pictured the Messiah as the righteous one, anointed of God, who would smite the enemies of Israel, and trample them to destruction. He would destroy the sinners from the face of the earth, he would disperse those who led the world astray. They conceived him not as an ordinary human being, but as one gifted with supernatural powers. He would reveal all the hidden treasures. They believed that the Messiah was pre-existent to creation; he would reveal himself in due time; he would be glorified and extolled by all the peoples of the earth. He would sit on the throne of his father, David. He would rule over his people, rewarding the pious and punishing the evil-doers. Thus, in the words of the *Book of Enoch*, the Messiah sits on the Throne of God: "For in those days, the Elect One shall arise and he shall choose the righteous and the holy from among them . . . and the Elect One shall in those days sit on My Throne."[39]

These, then, were the various parties, sects and philosophies that struggled against each other and against the Roman imperium in the Jewish state of the first century. The teachings of the *Sicarii* and the Apocalyptic-Pharisees were especially hateful to the Romans, for they were seditious and rebellious. Although these two groups were considered the same by Josephus, they were in truth hostile to each other. But the Romans made no distinction between them, the Romans crucified them alike.

It was at this time—a time of political, economic and religious strife—that Jesus of Nazareth preached his Sermon on the Mount. On his arrival in Jerusalem, he was hailed by his Jewish followers as "the son of David," "the King of the Jews." But a few short days later, Jesus was crucified by the Romans as "the King of the Jews."

CHAPTER VII

THE GOSPELS AS SOURCES

HITHERTO we have discussed the backgrounds as well as the social, economic and religious problems involved in a better understanding of the crucifixion of Jesus. We must now turn to the literary sources out of which we derive most, if not all, of our information concerning his trial, his controversies with the Pharisees, and his crucifixion. Of course, the sources are the Gospels, and these we must examine and evaluate.

1. ACCENT ON THEOLOGY

The Gospels are not primarily historical books. Their authors were not interested in the cold, historical facts. Not only were they not trained historians in our sense of the word, but the whole technique of writing history in the Jewish tradition was that of *tendenz*, or interpretative narration. Since the major concern of the Jewish mind was with the meaning of events and personalities from the point of view of divine intervention in human affairs, necessarily human history became the stage on which God played his role before the eyes of mankind. In a word, history was not the record of objective facts, so far as the human mind can be objective with what concerns the salvation of the soul, but became theological interpretation of "God's ways with man."

Thus, the Gospels reveal the theological accent upon

the events of Judea in the time of Jesus. They are
swathed about in theological clothes, and they are of
importance not only for the facts they contain, but for
the theological conceptions in which these facts are
bound up. The Gospels not only relate the events in
connection with Jesus' ministry and crucifixion, they
also convey the theological conceptions of the authors
about the place of Jesus in their religion. Thus, interpreting the messages of the ancient Hebrew prophets
in accordance with their notions, they believed Jesus to
be the Messiah Christ who would be crucified and resurrected as prophetically foretold.

The historian, therefore, if he is to attempt an objective account of the crucifixion of Jesus, must seek to
divorce the historical elements as recorded in the Gospels from their theological encasements. Fortunately,
there are four Gospels to aid the historian to ascertain
the historicity of certain events in the narrative of the
crucifixion. The first three (Matthew, Mark and Luke)
are known as "the Synoptic Gospels," as they are in
agreement generally each with the other. The fourth
Gospel (John), however, is known as "the non-Synoptic
Gospel," because it is, in many instances, in disagreement with the first three.

Moreover, the historian, because of the theological
accent, cannot rely on the accepted text describing the
trial and crucifixion of Jesus, and finds that an examination of the different manuscripts is indispensable. It
is well known that the various manuscripts of the New
Testament have different readings. While some readings may be due to inadvertent errors of the scribes,

we cannot overlook the fact that some readings reach back to an early period before the Gospels were actually put into writing.

Some versions in the Gospels, furthermore, may be ascribed to different schools of theology. The different translations of the New Testament from the Greek, and certain readings in the text itself, are revealing more from the point of view of theology than from the point of view of history. The translators apparently were more concerned with theology than with history. For they took no cognizance of the backgrounds of the times and the social forces of the Jewish state in which Jesus had his birth and lived.

Date of Crucifixion. In so important a matter as the date of the crucifixion of Jesus, there is a wide discrepancy between the Synoptic Gospels and the non-Synoptic Gospel. According to the first three Gospels, Jesus was crucified on the first day of Passover,[1] but, according to the non-Synoptic Gospel, he was crucified on the eve of Passover.[2] More concretely, from Matthew, Mark, and Luke, Jesus' Last Supper with his twelve disciples was "the Paschal Meal." It was on that night that Jesus was arrested, namely, the first night of Passover. And he was crucified on the morrow, the first day of Passover. According to John, however, Jesus was arrested on the night of the 13th of Nisan, the night before the first evening of Passover, and was crucified on the 14th of Nisan, *paresque* the eve of Passover, when "the Paschal Lamb" was slaughtered.

This discrepancy over so vitally important a matter as the very date of the crucifixion is strange, and many

scholars have tried variously to reconcile this contradiction. Most New Testament scholars are reduced to
the conviction that the sources are irreconcilable.[3] The
Gospels themselves being in such disagreement, it is
understandable why modern scholars likewise disagree
as to which contains the historical data—the Synoptic
Gospels or the non-Synoptic Gospel. However, some of
the modern scholars incline to the belief that the Gospel
according to John records the actual historical data,
and that Jesus was crucified on the eve of Passover. Accordingly, they believe the other three Gospels presuma-
bly "have blundered."[4]

Such mere opinion, however, cannot carry conclusive
weight. Not only is it necessary to choose the proper
source for the date of the crucifixion, but it is most
important to explain the divergence of the source material in respect to so momentous a matter.

According to tradition, Mark wrote down what he
heard from Peter.[5] If so, how, then, could he commit
such a blunder about the date of the crucifixion? The
eve of Passover and the first day of Passover are not ordinary occasions that easily slip from a Jew's memory;
they are days of the greatest solemnity in the Jewish
calendar. On the 14th of Nisan, the Jews brought the
"Paschal Lamb" to Jerusalem to be slaughtered. Later
in the evening they celebrated the "Paschal Meal" (the
Seder), with great festivity. The day following these
events was the first day of Passover. It is quite impossible for a Jew to confuse these different steps in the
celebration of his great festival. It is inconceivable that
Peter who participated in the Last Supper with his

Master, Jesus, should err. And as to Matthew, Mark, and Luke, how could they confuse such an important date? The very significance of the event—Jesus crucified as the Messiah—precludes the possibility of the trick of an erring memory; and these apostles were Jews; and these evangelists were aware of the full significance of the crucifixion and resurrection of Jesus.

Undoubtedly, the explanation of this confusion of dates lies in a different direction altogether. There is no real confusion of dates. There is difference of theological accent on events. The authors of the Gospels, in relating the historical events of the crucifixion of Jesus, represented different theological conceptions of Jesus as the Christ Messiah. The "Synoptic Gospels," on the one hand, conceived of Jesus *as the Saviour* personifying the idea of salvation in the Passover festival.[6] They emphasized the fact that he suffered death for the sins of the people, hence fulfilling, in his death and resurrection, the words of the prophets of Israel. Just as the Israelites were saved from the slavery of Egypt on the 15th day of Nisan, the first day of Passover, smearing the blood of "the Paschal Lamb" on their doors as a symbol of unity between God and Israel, so, according to the Gospels, the blood of Jesus served as a symbol of unity between God and the followers of Jesus.[7] On the other hand, the fourth Gospel presented the theological view of Jesus *as the Redeemer*, personifying the "Paschal Lamb." Just as the Paschal Lamb was sacrificed on the eve of Passover, so they conceived Jesus the Messiah to have been crucified on the eve of the Passover to redeem the world from Original Sin. The

Gospel according to John explicitly states: "Behold the Lamb of God which taketh away the sin of the world."[8] Furthermore, in narrating the crucifixion, John states that "when they came to Jesus, and saw that he was dead already, they brake not his legs."[9] It is quite evident that John had in mind the "Paschal Lamb" of which the Pentateuch wrote "a bone of him shall not be broken."[10]

Genealogy of Jesus. The date of the crucifixion of Jesus is not the only discrepancy between the Synoptic and non-Synoptic Gospels which may be traced to different theological motives. Indeed, even within the Synoptic Gospels themselves different theological interests may be discerned. This may be seen with especial clarity in connection with the genealogy of Jesus.

In giving the genealogy of Jesus as the son of David, the Gospels record two lists. Matthew traces the descent of Jesus from David through his son, Solomon. Luke, however, traces Jesus as a descendant of David through David's other son, Nathan. This is an impressive discrepancy within the Gospels themselves.

One reason advanced for these two differing genealogies of Matthew and Luke is that each had a different record. Even if this were so, the question still remains why did Luke ignore Solomon and his descendants, the kings of Judea, whose names are recorded in the books of the Hebrew prophets? Why should Luke record the names of descendants of Nathan, the son of David, names which are not recorded in the Bible?

Is not the true reason for these variations in genealogy to be found in this: that Luke had a theological reason for not giving Jesus' genealogical tree through Solomon? Solomon was the son of Bathsheba who had committed an adulterous act, something that Luke naturally would abhor. The Gospel of Luke, therefore, chose rather Nathan, the son of David, as the line of descent through which Jesus' ancestry was to be traced. Furthermore, Solomon and many of his descendants, the kings of Judea, were sinners, whose moral shortcomings were condemned by the ancient prophets themselves. Thus, the difference of the genealogical tree given by Luke in contrast to Matthew's was due to moral and theological reasons.

In evaluating the Gospels as source material for an understanding of the events of Jesus' life, trial and crucifixion, this discussion about the need to take into account the theological accent of the Gospels must not be overlooked.

2. FOR WHOM WRITTEN AND WHEN?

Another very important consideration in evaluating the Gospels as sources for our theme is to ascertain for whom they were written, and the date when they were written. An historian must keep in mind those for whom he writes. That he might make himself understood and convey with force and clarity the essential message he bears for his people, he must take into consideration their religious and theological apperceptive, the amount and quality of their knowledge. And each author, consciously or unconsciously, presents his case in terms and manner in which his audience can best understand him.

The authors of the Gospels wrote for Jewish Christians and Gentile Christians The early followers of Jesus were Jews who established a church in Jerusalem; these adherents of the new faith have come to be known as Jewish Christians. Later, many Gentiles accepted the teachings of Jesus; and these are named Gentile Christians. When the authors of the Gospels wrote, they had in mind either Jewish Christans or Gentile Christians, and accordingly framed their thoughts, their idioms, their very words.

Matthew and Luke. The consensus of opinion among the New Testament scholars is that the Gospel according to Matthew was written by a Jew for Jewish Christians.[11] The Gospel according to Luke was also written for Jewish Christians.[12] Their contents witness to the fact that they were written for the Jews. An example or two will suffice for the proof.

Both these Gospels insist on the observance of the Old Testament law, as Luke writes: "And it is easier for heaven and earth to pass than for one word of the law to fail." The Gospel according to Matthew says in the name of Jesus: "Think not that I am come to destroy the law (*Torah*), nor the Prophets. I am come not to destroy but to fulfill. For verily I say unto you, Till heaven and earth pass, one jot or one tittle shall in no wise pass from the law, till all be fulfilled." (Matt. 5:17-18) Both Luke and Matthew trace the genealogy of Jesus to King David, for they were writing for Jews who expected a Messiah descended from the family of David.

Gospel of Mark. In reference to the Gospel of Mark,

there are various opinions among New Testament scholars. Some maintain that this Gospel was written for
Gentiles.[13] They base their contention on the fact that
Mark uses explanatory remarks to elucidate Hebrew
terms, customs, and geographical places in Judea. However, this need not necessarily prove that Mark's audience consisted of Gentiles. The Gospel may, indeed,
have been composed for Jews, and his remarks may receive another interpretation altogether. The Jews of
the Diaspora were not well acquainted with the new
laws and customs which had been introduced in Jewish
life in Judea. Since early Christian tradition placed the
writing of this Gospel in Rome,[14] it is perfectly possible
that the author sought to clarify these laws and customs
for the Jews outside Judea. Since such Jews would not
be familiar with geographical and topographical places
of that country, the author felt the need of explaining
Judean geography and topography to them. Therefore,
there is no real reason to assume that the Gospel of
Mark was written for Gentile Christians.[15]

There is sufficient proof to hold that this Gospel, like
the other two mentioned above, was written for Jews.
Mark, like Matthew and Luke, quotes the words of
Jesus saying: "And Jesus said, 'I am: and ye shall see the
Son of man sitting on the right hand of power and
coming in the clouds of heaven.' "[16] The expression,
"the right hand of power," strikes one immediately as
being exceptional, for undoubtedly by "the right hand
of power" the author means "the right hand of God."
Now, in the *Tannaitic* literature the word *Geburah*,
"Power," is used as one of the names of God. Hence,

it is apparent that the author, knowing he was writing for Jews who would understand his use of this Hebrew idiom, felt free to describe "the right hand of God" as "the right hand of power." Thus, we may infer that the Gospel of Mark was written for Jews.

Mark[17] and Matthew and Luke relate that Peter wished to erect three tabernacles—one for Jesus, one for Moses, and one for Elias. In this way all three Gospels sought to assure a permanent position for the Jewish law in Christianity. This again sustains the opinion that Mark, as well as Matthew and Luke, was written for Jewish Christians.

Gospel of John. The Gospel according to John was written for Gentile Christians. Such expressions as relate to Jesus as "the Son of God" or the "Lamb of God," and the use of the word "your" in connection with the law reveal the audience for whom John wrote his words.

It is well known that the Gospel according to John does not lay stress on the idea that Jesus the Messiah was "the Son of David." This Gospel portrays Jesus as the "Lamb of God" or the "Son of God." The idea of the Messiah as the "Son of David" would hold no appeal for Gentile Christians. Therefore, John, writing for Gentile Christians, uses the phrase that would best reach their understanding.

In the Gospel of John, where controversies between Jesus and the Pharisees are described, the author has Jesus, when speaking to them, use the expression "your law" (your *Torah*). Likewise, in his disputes with the Jews, John has Jesus say "your law."[18] Now such a phrase does not occur in the Synoptic Gospels. Where, in the

Gospels of Matthew and Luke, the word "law" is mentioned—and that quite often—the words "your" and "their" are never appended to it. To be sure, in the narrative of the trial of Jesus, as recorded in the Synoptic Gospels, Pilate is made to say to the Jews, "Judge him according to your law"; but here this expression "your law" is perfectly natural, since it was the Roman procurator speaking to Jews; and, speaking to the Jews, it would be expected that he would address them with the words, "your law." With such exceptions, the Gospel of John, by its use of "your" and "their" in connection with the law, reveals that its message was directed to Gentile Christians.

While it is true that, in the Synoptic Gospels, the words "your tradition" is found in connection with the disputes between Jesus and the Pharisees, it must be recalled that the Synoptic Gospels were directed to Jewish Christians, who accepted the Bible as authoritative, but rejected the teachings of the sages or tradition. Hence, the use of the phrase "your tradition" in connection with the Pharisees is justifiable. On the other hand, the phrase "your law" (your *Torah*) and "their" law, as found in the Gospel according to John indicates quite clearly that this Gospel was intended for Gentile Christians.

Another example that might well demonstrate the nature of the people for whom the Gospels were written can be found in such phrases as the "Jewish Passover"[19] and the "Jewish Feast of Tabernacles."[20] These expressions are found only in the Gospel according to John and imply that this Gospel was intended for Gen-

tile Christians, for whom such a descriptive adjective
as "Jewish" might be necessary. The names "Passover"
and the "Feast of Unleavened Bread" are mentioned in
the Synoptic Gospels, but never with the word "Jewish."
Since they were written for Jewish Christians, the description "Jewish" would have been superfluous. In
general, it might be pointed out, in the Gospel according to John the name "Jews" is recorded over sixty
times, whereas in the Synoptic Gospels the name is
never mentioned, except in connection with pagans.

It is important to remember that, in evaluating the
Gospels as source material for a study of the trial of
Jesus and his times, not only the theological emphasis
be respected but the audience be considered also. And
finally, it is necessary to estimate the significance of the
Gospels according to the dates when they were written.

Date of the Gospels. The opinions of scholars have
for the most part agreed that the Gospels of Mark and
Matthew were written about 70 C.E.[21] The Gospel of
Luke was written some time after that period.[22] However, the Gospel of John cannot be placed earlier than
the year 100 C.E.[23] This theory is well supported both
by the general contents of the Gospels and by the expressions found in them.

The festival, for example, which is now known as
Passover, is called in the Bible the "Festival of Unleavened Bread." Now, the name "Passover" in the
Bible refers to the Paschal Lamb which was slaughtered
on the 14th day of Nisan. After the destruction of the
Temple, the name the "Festival of Unleavened Bread"
was still used, but the name "Passover" was increasingly

substituted for it. At a later date (a few decades after the destruction of the Temple), the name the "Festival of Unleavened Bread" was entirely abandoned, and the name of "Passover" was given both to the festival and to the Paschal Lamb. And to this day the festival is called *Pesah*—Passover.

Now, the Synoptic Gospels called this festival the "Feast of Unleavened Bread." This indicates that they were written not much after the destruction of the Temple. The Gospel of John, however, never used the name the "Feast of Unleavened Bread." The later expression "Passover" was used.[24] This fact clearly demonstrates that the Gospel of John was composed a number of decades after the destruction of the Temple.

Having established the audience for whom the Gospels were written and their dates, as well as the theological basis of their different interpretation of events, we now turn to a discussion of the Sermon on the Mount.

CHAPTER VIII

THE SERMON ON THE MOUNT

THE Sermon on the Mount which Jesus delivered some-
where in Galilee is considered by New Testament scholars to be a great spiritual message given to mankind.
It provides the basis of Christianity's ethical and religious manifesto to humanity. Many New Testament
scholars believe that the ethical values of the Sermon
on the Mount are superior to the ethics of Judaism.
The general conviction is held that Jesus in his Sermon opposed the teachings of the Pentateuch, and thus
undermined its validity as an ethical way of life. To
establish this theory of Jesus' hostility to the Pentateuch
the following passage in the Sermon on the Mount has
become classic:

Ye have heard that it hath been said, An eye for an eye,
and a tooth for a tooth: But I say unto you, That ye
resist not evil: but whosoever shall smite thee on the right
cheek, turn to him the other also. And if any man will sue
thee at the law, and take away thy coat, let him have thy
cloak, also. And whosoever shall compel thee to go a mile,
go with him twain. Give to him that asketh thee, and
from him that would borrow of thee turn not thou away.[1]

This theory, however, cannot be justified. Jesus could
not have been opposed to the Pentateuch, for he himself asserted, "Think not I am come to destroy the law,
or the prophets: I am not come to destroy but to fulfill.
For verily I say unto you, Till heaven and earth pass,

one jot or one tittle shall in no wise pass from the law till all be fulfilled."[2]

Moreover, it might be asked, how could Jesus be against the Bible? His entire mission on earth as the Messiah, descended from David, and as the "Son of God" was based on the validity of the Bible. How could he oppose one set of Biblical teachings and uphold another set of teachings? He had to maintain the authority of the Bible in its entirety to fulfill its ultimate divine goal. The question therefore remains: what was the meaning of Jesus' statement, "Ye have heard that it hath been said, An eye for an eye, and a tooth for a tooth: But I say unto you. . . ."

The storm center of the controversy revolves about the so-called *lex talionis*, or as it is sometimes referred to, the law of *talio*, that is the law of "An eye for an eye, etc." Lately much has been written about the law of *talio*, about its harshness, its cruelty, its inhumanness. Some try to prove the superiority of the ethical teachings of the Gospels over those of the Bible, because of *talio*. Many scholars, on the other hand, both Jewish and Christian, have sought to prove that in reality the *lex talionis* was never practiced among the Jews during the time of Jesus. Granted that the Bible says, "An eye for an eye, etc.," yet, in actuality, this *Halakah* (law) was never applied in the Jewish state. And hence, no inferences from this text can provide proof that the ethical teachings of Jesus were superior to the Jewish teachings of his day. But, first it is necessary to comprehend the meaning and use of the Biblical law, "An eye for an eye." And to this end we must at the outset analyze the Biblical laws relating to public and private wrongs.

1. PUBLIC AND PRIVATE WRONGS

We must keep in mind that the ancients had conceptions of the nature of crime and wrong, and the place of the state in their punishment which were different from our own. Many wrongs which today are considered crimes against the state and which the state is empowered to punish were, in ancient times, not so regarded. They were held to be crimes and wrongs done by individuals against individuals in which punishment rested in the hands of the individuals wronged or in the hands of the family or tribe to which he belonged. The state, or the community as a whole was not given the right to interpose itself and wreak punishment on the culprit.

The Bible, as well as the ancient Roman law, considered *furtum* (theft) and injuries as *private delict*,[3] that is, the state had no right to interfere in such matters; they were private wrongs. The *actio furti*, that is the action against the doer of the wrong, was done by the person injured, not by the state, as is the practice in our modern law. There were public crimes and wrongs in which the state had the right to prosecute the evildoer. In cases like cursing God, or worshiping foreign gods, or adultery, and, in the Bible, desecrating the Sabbath openly, the state was empowered to bring charges against the offender, prosecute him, and even put him to death, if proved guilty. These were crimes not against an individual but against the state as state.

And, many wrongs and crimes which today we regard
as done against the state, were in those days considered
private matters. Let us consider such wrongs as homicide, theft and personal injury.

Homicide. Homicide was not considered a crime
against the state. In primitive society, the kin of the
family was supposed to avenge the death of any members of the tribe by killing the murderer.

In time it was realized that murder sometimes resulted from accident. Since murder might occur without intention to kill, Moses legislated the creation of
"Cities of Refuge" to which the slayer might flee, if he
were innocent, and thus prevent himself from being
slain by the "Avenger of the Blood" of the slain. If the
slayer could prove that the victim was killed by accident, and that he was not his enemy at all, then he remained in the "City of Refuge" until the death of the
high priest. The authorities of the city had no right to
deliver him over to the "Avenger of the Blood."

If it was later proved, however, that the accused had
deliberately killed the man, the authorities were required to deliver him to the "Avenger of the Blood"
who then had the right and duty to slay him.[4]

Thus, from the description given in the Bible concerning homicide, we may safely say that homicide was
not considered a crime against the state, but against the
family of the victim, and hence, the kin of the family
had to avenge the murder. The authorities had only to
decide whether the murder was accidental or deliberate.
The execution of the criminal was carried out by the
"Avenger of the Blood." Of course, there were border-

line cases where rights and duties of individual and state overlapped. Therefore, apparently Moses could not entirely exclude all cases of homicide from the jurisdiction of the tribes, but had to adjust custom and law, and make compromises. He limited the power of the tribes by instituting the "Cities of Refuge."

That the institution of the "Avenger of the Blood" was still in force during the First Temple we have no definite proof. But, from the story recorded in II Samuel, we may infer that it did operate in those days. It is recorded there that Joab killed Abner for the blood of Asahel, his brother, which may mean that Joab was really acting as the "Avenger of the Blood."[5]

After the Jews returned from Babylon, however, the institution of the "Avenger of the Blood" was abolished. And, since the Jews were no longer divided into tribes, the "Cities of Refuge" also disappeared. But, in order to take care of all cases of homicide, the state later established a court to this end, the Sanhedrin. During the period of the Second Jewish Commonwealth, homicide was considered a crime against society and not against the individual or the family. And society, not the individual, was empowered to punish the offender.

Theft. According to the Bible, *furtum* (theft), was considered *private delict*. If a man had stolen property from his fellow man, he had to pay a fine to the owner of the property. If it was an ox, he had to pay double the value of the beast; but if he had sold or slaughtered the ox, he had to pay a fine of five times its value; for a sheep, fourfold. From the Bible, as well as from the *Tannaitic* literature, we learn that only the man who was injured could demand a fine from the thief. The state had no power to interfere. It was a matter entirely between the offender and the man who suffered the loss.

Injury and mutilation. Injury and bodily mutilation, likewise, were considered private wrongs. The sufferer had the right to fix the punishment, and if he lost an eye or a tooth, he possessed the right to take out an eye or a tooth from the offender. The Twelve Tables of the ancient Roman Law provided that bodily mutilation was punishable by the law of *talio.*

The law of *talio,* as it is described in the Bible, was not for the state to enforce, since the action was not considered a crime against society, and the state was not empowered to interfere, or to punish the offender. It was a case between the person who inflicted the injury and the man who was injured. The man who suffered could entirely absolve the man who caused the injury from punishment, or he could demand any satisfaction he desired, even to taking out the eye of the man who caused the loss of his eye. *Talio* was the ultimate and extreme satisfaction which the plaintiff could exact. However, he might take his satisfaction with money. He was the sole judge.

Josephus bears out this interpretation of the law of *talio* when he says:

He that maimeth any one, let him undergo the like himself, and be deprived of the same member of which he hath deprived the other, unless he that is maimed will accept of money instead of it; for the law makes the sufferer the judge of the value of what he hath suffered,

and permits him to estimate it unless he will be more
severe.[6]

From this statement it is quite obvious that Josephus
considered injury as a *private delict*, that is, a matter
between the injured and the offender.

The attitudes of the Pharisees and of Jesus toward
the law of *talio* in a changing social world reveal the
essential difference between them in many of their controversies over Jewish laws and customs. In the early
days of the Second Jewish Commonwealth, the Pharisees felt the need of abolishing the *lex talionis*, and
they did in reality abolish it. This was done by a
legal fiction which limited the right of the man who
suffered the loss of an eye to take out an eye exactly
like his own in size and color.[7] Since it was impossible
for two men to have precisely the same organs in every
respect, the injured could not make use of the law of
talio. Thus, by this legal fiction, the law of *talio* was in
reality abolished. The injured man had the right only
to demand monetary satisfaction for the loss of his eye,
for the pain, for medical care, for disability and for
humiliation.

When, on the other hand, Jesus said, concerning the
law of *talio*, "It has been said, An eye for an eye, but I
say unto you, Resist no evil," he spoke as a moralist,
appealing to the people that they should not only not
demand satisfaction by *talio*, but that they should not
resist evil at all. "Whosoever shall smite thee on thy
right cheek, turn to him the other also." Moreover, he
could not refer to the Jewish state, for the state, as has

been pointed out, had no right to inflict the punishment "An eye for an eye." Jesus referred to individuals. In a word, the essential difference between Jesus and the Pharisees lay in this: The Pharisees abolished *talio* by legal fiction, making it impossible for the plaintiff to demand an eye for an eye, while Jesus appealed to the conscience of the plaintiff not to demand an eye for an eye and not to resist evil by repaying evil. The Pharisees relied on legal interpretation, whereas Jesus sought to exert moral influence.

But the point to be emphasized is that Jesus neither by his attitude nor by his exhortation, preached against the Pentateuch. He respected the law of *talio* as stated in the Pentateuch, but he appealed to the ethical conscience of individuals not to use the right that was given them by the Pentateuch.

2. ETHICS VERSUS LAW

Jesus approached the problems of his day purely as an ethical teacher. He disregarded the state, and based his teachings on the individual. He made ethical appeals, seeking the reconstruction of innate human nature. The Pharisees, on the other hand, without denying the ethical goals of Jesus, had to approach these problems in terms of social realities, for they bore the responsibility for the peace and welfare of society and state. They sought these ethical goals by means of the social controls provided by law and its interpretation. The Pharisees, who were members of the religious Sanhedrin, had to interpret the Pentateuchal laws by which society was to be governed. Jesus was not interested in applying the laws by which society was to be governed. As an ethical teacher, he appealed to the consciences of people to abstain from any evil so that there would be no necessity for courts and judges. According to Jesus, when in the Pentateuch we find punishment for evil-doing, he attributed the evil to the fact that man's nature was bad. By changing his nature, there would be no need for punishment. In a word, the Pharisees presented law as an instrument of ethical living, while Jesus relied entirely on ethics and ethical exhortation to change human nature. With this point of view in mind we can better understand the other teachings of Jesus in his Sermon on the Mount, and his other differences with the Pharisees.

Divorce. Jesus said: "It hath been said, whosoever shall put away his wife, let him give her a writing of divorcement: But I say unto you, that whosoever shall put away his wife, saving for the cause of fornication, causeth her to commit adultery: and whosoever shall marry her that is divorced committeth adultery."[8]

Here again, Jesus was not opposed to the Pentateuchal law that a man may give a bill of divorce, but his opinion was that Mosaic permission to divorce was due to sin, and not to the original plan of man's creation, where it was indicated that man and wife should be as one flesh. Therefore, Jesus was against divorce except in the case of adultery; and he believed that the person who married a divorcee was committing an act of adultery.

This is clear from the following statement of Jesus: "They say unto him, why did Moses then command to give a writ of divorcement, and to put her away? He saith unto them, Moses, because of the hardness of your hearts, suffered you to put away your wives: but from the beginning it was not so. And I say unto you, Whosoever shall put away his wife, except it be for fornication, and shall marry another, committeth adultery: and whoso marrieth her which is put away doth commit adultery."[9]

The difference between Jesus and the Pharisees in the question of divorce may be summed up in this way: According to Jesus, Moses permitted divorce because of the hardness of the hearts of men which was due to sin, and not to the original plan of man's creation, where it is written that they should become one flesh. The Pharisees (the School of Hillel), on the other hand, granted that the original intention was that they should be one flesh, but they maintained that, in reality, the original plan of man's creation, symbolized as "one flesh," does not work out where the husband no longer cares for his wife (or, as R. Akiba puts it, he has found a woman he likes better).[10] The Pharisees believed that, under such circumstances, it is better that they separate, and they permitted the husband to divorce his wife.

The Pharisees resorted to interpreting the law to ameliorate marital conditions; Jesus, attributing such marital conditions to sin, sought, rather, to reconstruct sinning human nature.

Adultery. Jesus said: "Ye have heard that it was said by them of old time, Thou shalt not commit adultery: But I say unto you, That whosoever looketh on a woman to lust after her hath committed adultery with her already in his heart. And if thy right eye offend thee, pluck it out, and cast it from thee: for it is profitable for thee that one of thy members should perish, and not that thy whole body should be cast into Gehenna."[11]

The Pharisees, as members of the religious Sanhedrin, would punish a person only when he committed an actual act of adultery, but they would not punish a man for his mere intention. Although the Pharisees considered the coveting of a woman as a sin, this sin, however, could not be punished by a court, but would be punished by God. The Pharisees held themselves strictly within the bounds of the law.

Jesus, on the other hand, as an ethical teacher, had regard for the inner motive. He maintained that to covet a woman in one's heart is as much a sin as to commit the act of adultery itself. Therefore, according to him, "if thy right eye offend thee, pluck it out, and cast it from thee." Jesus moved in the realm of ethical motivations.

Oaths. In the Sermon on the Mount Jesus said: "Again ye have heard that it was said by them of old time, Thou shalt not forswear thyself, but shalt perform unto the Lord thine oaths: But I say unto you, Swear not at all."

According to the Pentateuch, if a man made a promise, he must pay his oath to God.[12] Jesus, however, maintained that a man has no right to swear at all.

The Pharisees concerned themselves with a man's carrying out his obligation, once he had assumed it. Jesus was concerned that a man should forswear undertaking obligations. The former brought oaths within

the realm of law; Jesus was intent upon the ethical
question of taking oaths at all.

Anger. The conflict between ethics and law is again
revealed by Jesus when he says: "Ye have heard it was
said to the ancients, Thou shalt not commit murder,
and whosoever shall do so, shall be in danger of the
judgment. But I say unto you, That every one who is
angry with his brother shall be liable to the judgment,
and whosoever shall say to his brother, Raca, shall be
liable to the Sanhedrin, but whosoever shall say, thou
fool, shall be liable to the Gehenna of fire."

According to Pentateuchal law, only an act is liable
to judicial prosecution. If a man committed murder,
he was liable to the judgment. But, according to Jesus,
even for harboring inner feelings of doing violence, a
man is liable to the judgment of God. Once more we
see clearly the opposition between law and ethics.

The moral teachings of Jesus as antithetic to law and
the nature of mankind reveal their impracticality in
his teaching of the Sermon on the Mount: "Ye have
heard that it hath been said, Thou shalt love thy neighbor and hate thine enemy. But I say unto you, Love
your enemies, bless them that curse you, do good to
them that hate you, and pray for them which despite-
fully use you and persecute you." It must be pointed
out that the saying "hate thine enemy" does not occur
either in the Bible or in the *Tannaitic* literature.[13]

According to Jesus, a man is supposed not only to
love his neighbor but also to love his enemy. In the
light of this ethical teaching, one is impelled to ask this
question: If a man breaks into my home and kills my

children, am I to love this murderer? I can understand the need to desist from seeking revenge. I can even be persuaded of the justice of not killing the culprit without a fair trial to ascertain whether the crime was done intentionally or unintentionally. I might even restrain my feelings from hating him who may be mentally unbalanced or the unfortunate victim of circumstances over which he has no control. But to ask me to love him, though he slew my children, approaches the humanly impossible.

Jesus, the ethical teacher, either did not fully comprehend the nature of human beings, or else he wanted his Sermon on the Mount to be a utopian standard toward which mankind should strive. Judging our civilization by the history of the last two millenniums, we may say that it is possible for a man to love his friend; that it may even be possible not to despise his enemy; but it is totally impossible for him to love his enemy.

The ethical teachings of the Sages are far more practicable than those of Jesus. Hillel said: "What thou hatest for thyself, do not do to thy fellow man."[14] Similarly, the author of the Book of Tobit writes: "What thou thyself hatest, do to no man."[15] These teachings of the Sages may not be superior to those of Jesus, but they are more in accordance with the realities of human nature, and lie within the realm of possibilities where human beings strive to achieve a better individual and social life.

Viewing human history in the perspective of the ages, we cannot help but conclude that Jesus' teachings are not followed even by his own flock, the professing

Christians. Nineteen centuries after Jesus' advent, his ideas of love and equality between man and man are not yet within the possibility of fulfillment. Men are not only not ready for the Messianic age, but hatred that is bitter and deep still exists in the hearts of his followers. People hate their fellow men, not because they have committed wrongs against them, but because they hold different ideas about the state, about political, religious or economic matters. The Kingdom of Heaven upon earth is still as far away now as it was in the days of Jesus, when he preached equality between man and man, and love for all, even for his enemies.

Our analysis of the teachings of Jesus in his Sermon on the Mount reveals the essential and basic difference between Jesus and the Pharisees. The Pharisees, members of the religious Sanhedrin, and hence the spiritual leaders of the Jewish people, although maintaining that ethical teachings are of paramount importance for the reshaping of human nature, insisted on the fulfillment of the law, always conscious of the need for equity in the law. They held to the conviction that a state cannot exist unless it is maintained by law and order. Jesus, on the other hand, not being interested in the state, could appeal to his fellow men in purely ethical terms, relying on moral exhortation, saying: "That ye resist not evil: but whosoever shall smite thee on thy right cheek, turn to him the other also."

CHAPTER IX

JESUS' CONTROVERSIES WITH THE PHARISEES

THE Synoptic Gospels tell us of controversies and conflicts between Jesus and the Pharisees. What were the underlying motives of those conflicts? Did not Jesus follow the doctrines of the Pharisees on reward and punishment, that the wicked would be punished in the future world and the pious would be rewarded? Did he not follow the belief of the Pharisees in resurrection, that the righteous would be resurrected? Did not the Pharisees believe in a Messiah, that a scion of David would rule over the Jews? Why, then, did they engage in such heated arguments?

Before answering these questions, we shall first present the account as given in the Synoptic Gospels:

At that time Jesus went on the sabbath day through the corn; and his disciples were an hungred, and began to pluck the ears of corn, and to eat. But when the Pharisees saw it, they said unto him, Behold, thy disciples do that which is not lawful to do upon the sabbath day. But he said unto them, Have ye not read what David did, when he was an hungred, and they that were with him; how he entered into the house of God, and did eat the shewbread, which was not lawful for him to eat, neither for them which were with him, but only for the priests? Or have ye not read in the Torah how that on the sabbath days the priests in the Temple profane the sabbath and are blameless? But I say unto you, That in this place is one greater than the Temple. But if ye had known what this meaneth, I will have mercy, and not sacrifice, ye would not have condemned the guiltless. For the Son of man is Lord even of the sabbath day.[1]

1. JESUS AND THE SABBATH

According to the Bible, no work can be done on the Sabbath day. However, sacrifices were brought to the Temple on the Sabbath and the priests performed their duties on this day. This was not considered profaning the Sabbath since it was connected with the Temple. It was pointed out previously that the Pharisees, likewise, permitted the Israelites to work on the Sabbath if the work was intended for the Temple.[2] They also permitted the profanation of the Sabbath in order to save a man's life. Jesus and his disciples went on the Sabbath day to the cornfields where his disciples plucked the ears of corn to eat. Jesus claimed dispensation from the Pentateuchal law which prohibited work on the Sabbath on the ground that he was a priest, the son of David, and hence, "Lord even of the sabbath day." Jesus further contested the Pharisees by saying: "Have ye not read what David did, when he was an hungred and they that were with him; how he entered into the house of God and did eat the shewbread, which was not lawful for him to eat?"

The Pharisees, on the other hand, believed that David ate of the bread in the Temple to save his life, but the disciples of Jesus did not eat the ears of the corn to save their lives. The Pharisees neither believed that Jesus was a priest nor that his work was connected with the Temple. They rejected him as the "Son of Man" and hence, he was not the "Lord of the sabbath."

The Pharisees were always ready to amend the laws of the Sabbath and to make it possible for the people to observe the Sabbath. That the Sabbath was made for man and not man for the Sabbath was the contention of the Pharisees.[3] They also objected to Jesus' healing on the Sabbath because they did not believe that Jesus knew the art of healing. It is true that the Pharisees allowed medical treatment to be performed where life was at stake, but the Pharisees did not believe in Jesus' power to heal. And when Jesus, indeed, according to the Gospels, restored one man's hand to its strength, the Pharisees—according to the same authority—accused Jesus of doing this with the power of the "chief of the devils," that he cast out the devils by Beelzebub, chief of the devils.[4]

2. JESUS AND FASTING

This denial of the Pharisees that Jesus was the Messiah, the son of David, is reflected in another controversy recorded in the Synoptic Gospels:

And John's disciples and the Pharisees were fasting: and they come and say unto him, Why do John's disciples and the disciples of the Pharisees fast, but thy disciples fast not? And Jesus said unto them, Can the sons of the bride-chamber fast, while the bridegroom is with them? As long as they have the bridegroom with them they cannot fast. But the days will come when the bridegroom shall be taken away from them, and then will they fast in that day.[5]

Fasting among the Jews was quite common. We are told David fasted when his child was sick[6] and that R. Zaddok fasted for forty years to ward off the destruction of the Temple.[7] Fasting was always considered one of the principle means of alleviation of calamities. Likewise, in time of public suffering, like drought, public fasts were decreed. This controversy again centered on the point that Jesus claimed to be the Messiah, a scion of the house of David. Hence, his disciples were not supposed to observe the national fast days which were connected with the destruction of the first Temple. From the Bible we learn that upon the restoration of the Jewish state, the people asked the Prophet Zechariah if they should continue to fast on the days that were instituted in commemoration of the destruction of the first Temple. The Prophet Zechariah answered the Jews in the name of God in these words: "The fast of the Fourth month and the fast of the Fifth, and the fast of the Seventh and the fast of the Tenth, shall be to the House of Judah joy and gladness and cheerful feasts."[8]

This, however, does not indicate that the Jews did not continue to fast on those days during the Second Commonwealth. The prophecy of Zechariah was not fulfilled and the Jews had no occasion to abrogate those fasts and declare them to be cheerful feasts. Not all the Jews had returned to Palestine. The kingdom of David had not been restored. On the contrary, the Jews suffered first under the Greeks and then under the Romans. Neither King Jannaeus Alexander nor Herod were ideal kings and, therefore, they had no reason to rejoice and to abandon the fasts.

From Josephus we know that the Jews continued to
fast on those days during the Second Commonwealth
in memory of the destruction of their kingdom. Pompey
captured Jerusalem on the ninth of Tammuz—a fast
day in commemoration of the fall of Jerusalem to the
Babylonians.[9] To the accusation of the Pharisees that
Jesus' disciples did not observe the national fast days,
Jesus replied: "Can the sons of the bride-chamber fast,
while the bridegroom is with them? As long as they have
the bridegroom with them they cannot fast. But the
days will come when the bridegroom shall be taken
from them, and then will they fast in that day." By
this parable Jesus meant to say that his disciples need
not fast, as He, the Messiah, was among them and,
therefore, the fast days in memory of the destruction
of the Temple need not be observed. "But the days will
come when the bridegroom shall be taken from them,
and then they will fast in that day." That is to say,
when Jesus shall be taken away, his followers will fast.

3. WASHING THE HANDS, AND THE CORBAN

The controversies between the Pharisees and Jesus
were not only concerned with the fact that they did
not recognize Jesus as the Messiah; and hence, that he
had no claim for dispensation from the Biblical law.
They also contested his unprecedented actions, for he
did not observe the traditions of the elders, the laws
which the Pharisees enacted.

The Gospels of Mark and Matthew tell us that there
was contention between the Pharisees and Jesus about
the institution of washing the hands and the corban:

Then came together unto him the Pharisees and certain
of the scribes, which came from Jerusalem. And when they
saw some of his disciples eat bread with defiled, that is to
say, with unwashen hands, they found fault. For the Pharisees and all the Jews, except they wash their hands oft,
eat not, holding the tradition of the Elders . . . Then the
Pharisees and scribes asked him, Why walk not thy disciples
according to the tradition of the Elders, but eat bread
with unwashen hands? He answered and said unto them,
Well hath Esaias prophesied of you "hypocrites," as is
written, This people honoureth me with their lips, but
their heart is far from me. Howbeit in vain do they worship me, teaching for doctrines the commandments of
men. For laying aside the commandment of God, ye hold
the tradition of men, as the washing of pots and cups;
and many other such like things ye do. And he said unto
them, Full well ye reject the commandment of God, that
ye may keep your own tradition. For Moses said, Honour
thy father and thy mother, and Whoso curseth father or
mother, let him die the death. But ye say, if a man shall
say to his father or mother, It is Corban (that is a gift) by
whatsoever thou mightest be profited by me, he shall be
free. And ye suffer him no more to do aught for his
father or his mother; Making the word of God of none
effect through your tradition, which ye have delivered:
and many such like things do ye.[10]

Washing the Hands. In the previous pages,[11] the underlying reasons for the enactment of the institution of
washing the hands before meals were explained. The
Pharisees introduced this law in order to ease the bur-
dens of the laws of purity and impurity upon the people. The disciples of Jesus ate without washing their
hands. They denied the tradition of the elders.

Jesus countercharged that they themselves, the Pharisees, were rejecting the laws of God in upholding their own tradition. For it is written in the Pentateuch, he said, "Honour thy father and thy mother." And the Pharisees maintained that if a man took a *corban*, a vow,[12] not to honor his father or his mother, he must keep that vow. By this Jesus claimed the Pharisees themselves were nullifying the Pentateuchal law of God.

In these charges and countercharges is reflected the philosophy of the Pharisees and Jesus concerning the nature of society. The Pharisees were the leaders of the religious Sanhedrin. As such, they had to take cognizance of the weaknesses of human nature, knowing that a person may transgress a precept; and therefore, it was their duty to find a way to give the person the opportunity for repentance and readjustment. Jesus, on the other hand, believed a person should be taught that he should never transgress the laws, not taking into consideration the weakness of humanity.

The corban, the vow. According to the Pharisees a vow must be kept since it is written in the Pentateuch that a man should not break his word. But if a man took a vow against the Biblical precept he must keep his vow, and not observe the precept for which, according to them, he would be punished for not observing the precept. However, to avoid a clash between two commandments in the Pentateuch, namely, "Honour thy father and thy mother" and "He shall not break his word," the Pharisees introduced a legal fiction. If a man took a vow not to honor his father and his mother, he could absolve himself of his vow. This is called, in the *Tannaitic* literature, the "invalidation of vows."[13] According to Jesus, however, no vow could be taken against a Pentateuchal precept, thus disregarding human weakness that a man might transgress, and take a vow against a Pentateuchal precept.

4. JESUS, THE PUBLICANS AND THE SINNERS

According to the Synoptic Gospels, the Pharisees objected to Jesus for his association with publicans and sinners, "And when the Pharisees saw it, they said unto his disciples, Why eateth your Master with publicans and sinners?"[14] The reason why the Pharisees did not want to break bread with the sinners was not due to pride or to exclusiveness. For the Pharisees, the table was not merely a place for eating and drinking and satisfying their human needs but it was as well a place for learned discussion and prayers. Again, it was very hard for the Pharisees, who observed the laws of purity and impurity, to eat with sinners who were neither versed in the laws of purity and impurity, nor observed them.

Jesus, on the other hand, denied the "Tradition of the Elders," and hence did not observe the laws of purity and impurity according to the Pharisees' conception. He could, therefore, associate with the sinners by eating with them.

The Pharisees, likewise, resented the fact that Jesus associated with the publicans. The publicans were considered not only robbers, since they collected taxes from the Jews for their oppressors, the Romans; they were also considered as traitors to their people by help-

ing the Romans to subjugate the Jews. The pious and
patriotic Jews did not associate with them. Jesus who
was likewise opposed to the Romans for the enslavement of the Jews and who was hailed by his followers
as the king of the Jews, however associated with the
publicans. He thought that by personal contact with,
and by preaching to and teaching the publicans, they
would repent and give up their evil way of life. Jesus,
seeking a new ethical social order, looked for help from
the slums, and the lower classes of society, the "un-
touchables," and from them he drew his followers.

There are interesting stories, reminiscent of the actions of Jesus, recorded about the founder of the mystic
religious sect in the eighteenth century known by the
name *Hasidism* (not to be confused with the *Hasidim*
of the Second Commonwealth). We are told that Rabbi
Israel Baal-Shem-Tob (BeShT), the founder of the
Hasidic sect, associated himself only with the lowest
classes of Jewish society. He was always found in company with sinners and thieves and those who transgressed the Rabbinical law. The Rabbis, like the earlier
Pharisees, looked down upon Israel Baal-Shem-Tob
with scorn.

A story is told in the name of Rabbi Israel BeShT
which resembles very much some of the stories in the
Gospels. For example, a married woman committed
adulterous acts with her serf. When her two brothers
became aware of her conduct, they decided to kill her.
In order to dispose of her, they invited her to their
home. Through divine inspiration it became known to

Rabbi Israel BeShT. He went to the place and saved her, and she became a pious woman.[15]

5. WERE THE PHARISEES "HYPOCRITES"?

The accusation of the Pharisees by Jesus of hypocrisy was not justifiable. Their interpretations of the laws were not a burden upon the people, as Jesus charged. The Pharisees always strove to make the *Halakah* (laws) easy for the people. They themselves were the people. The Pharisees always endeavored to bring the *Halakah* into consonance with life, and they amended the Pentateuchal law to meet life's demands. The Pharisees were always ready to harmonize religion and life, and indeed brought about many reforms in the Jewish religion.

It has already been pointed out that some people, who, for designing reasons called themselves Pharisees, acted contrary to Pharisaic teachings. The Pharisees themselves condemned such men and always advised the people to be on their guard against these pretenders. It is possible that Jesus had in mind this kind of Pharisee. It is probable that the author of the *Assumption of Moses* referred to this kind of Pharisee, when he said:

And in the time of these, destructive and impious men shall rule, saying that they are just . . . Devourers of the goods of the (poor) saying that they do so on the ground of their justice, but in reality to destroy them, complainers, deceitful, concealing themselves lest they should be recognized, impious, filled with lawlessness and iniquity from sunrise to sunset, saying: "We shall have feastings and luxury, eating and drinking, and we shall esteem ourselves as princes."[16] However, the *Assumption of Moses* was composed in the year 140 C.E. and therefore could not have referred to the Pharisees. The author of this passage had in mind the leaders of the Bar Kokba revolt.

It cannot be denied that the disciples of Jesus were sharply opposed to the Pharisees and had many arguments with them. It is quite likely that in the heat of the arguments they accused the Pharisees, their former teachers, of being hypocrites, for not accepting Jesus as the Messiah. It is a matter of general experience that people who hold common beliefs in religion, or common ideas in politics or in economics, often attack each other more bitterly than people who have nothing in common. The Pharisees, through their teachings, were responsible for the ideas which brought about Christianity. The Pharisees with their ideas about the future world and reward and punishment and Providence made possible the teachings of Jesus and his disciples. There was no great resentment shown against the Sadducees, since they had nothing in common with the disciples of Jesus, nor with their people.

There is even a possibility that the words "Pharisees, hypocrites" never came from the mouth of Jesus. They were interpolated later. As a matter of fact, the words in Mark 7:6 "you hypocrites" are not found in some manuscripts. Likewise, in Luke 13:15 the word "hypocrite" does not occur in some of the manuscripts. The harsh words used by Jesus against the Pharisees are mostly found in chapter 23 of Matthew, like "Woe unto you Scribes and Pharisees Hypocrites." It may be questioned whether Jesus actually said this.

6. THE TITLE "RABBI"

The expression "Rabbi" as a technical name occurs several times in this chapter (Matthew 23). The word "Rabbi" as a technical expression was not used by the Jews until the destruction of the Second Temple. The scholars used their own names but never affixed to them the title "Rabbi," for example Hillel, Simon, etc.

Only with the advent of Gamaliel, the title "Rabban" was affixed which meant "our Master." The reason was that up to the time of Gamaliel two men presided over the Sanhedrin, one the *Nasi* and the other the *Ab-bet-din*. In the time of Gamaliel the position of *Ab-bet-din* was abolished, and entire authority was vested in Gamaliel alone. Hence, the title given him was *Rabban*, "Master." The word *Rabban* is derived from *Rab* meaning "elder," "master." At the time of the destruction of the Second Temple, the title "Rabbi" was given to all scholars who received authorization to decide the law. Hence, it is surprising to read that Jesus was given the title of Rabbi, when in his time, such a title was not yet used.[17]

The word "Rabbi" which is found in this chapter may, therefore, throw light on the authenticity of the entire chapter. Jesus was usually addressed as *didaskale* (Teacher). Even when the Pharisees and the "Scholars of the Law" addressed him, they always called him Teacher and not Rabbi.[18] We, therefore, expect that the Pharisees and the "Scholars of the Law," when they asked Jesus questions on the law, would have addressed him as Rabbi, if such a title had then been in vogue.

In the story of the betrayal of Judas Iscariot, the expression "Rabbi" also occurs. The Gospel according to Matthew tells us, "Now he that betrayed him gave them a sign saying, Whomsoever I shall kiss, that same is he: hold him fast. And forthwith he came to Jesus and said, Hail, Rabbi, and kissed him."[19] The same account is given in the Gospel according to Mark. In the account given in the Gospel according to Luke, the word "Rabbi" is missing. "And while he yet spake, behold a multitude and he that was called Judas, one of the twelve, went before them, and drew near unto Jesus to kiss him."[20]

The Gospel according to John gives an entirely different version of Judas' betrayal of Jesus. He does not follow the account that is given in the Synoptic Gospels about Judas' betrayal of Jesus by a kiss, but according to him, Judas knew the place where Jesus met his disciples and led the officers to arrest Jesus. Thus, we see that the word "Rabbi" in connection with the tale of Judas is found only in Matthew and Mark, but is missing in Luke. John gives an altogether different version. We may, therefore, assume that the word "Rabbi," found in the first two Gospels, was interpolated later.

7. ANIMOSITY AGAINST PHARISEES AND JEWS

The name "Pharisees" is mentioned many times in the Gospel of John. Unlike the Synoptic Gospels, we do not find in John any animosity toward the Pharisees. Neither do we find the phrase "Pharisees, hypocrites." One man named Nicodemus, a Pharisee, even joined

Jesus. According to John, some of the Pharisees even admitted that Jesus performed miracles, hence he could not be a sinner.[21] From the same Gospel we learn that some of the rulers of the Synagogue believed in Jesus, but they did not have the courage to confess their belief openly.[22]

In John 7 we are told that the leaders and the Pharisees sent officers to bring Jesus to them. The officers, however, returned without Jesus. Thereupon, the Pharisees reproached them for returning without him. The officers answered, "Never man spake like this man. Then answered them the Pharisees, 'Are ye also deceived? Have any of the rulers of the Pharisees believed on him? But these people who knoweth not the law are cursed.' Nicodemus saith unto them 'Doth our law judge any man before it hear him, and know what he doeth?' "[23] Even in this story we do not find the great animosity between the Pharisees and Jesus that is found throughout the Synoptic Gospels. The hostility in this Gospel is directed against the Jews as a whole.

How can we explain this difference in attitude toward the Pharisees in the Synoptic Gospels and in the Gospel of John? The difference in attitude is undoubtedly due to the distinctive audiences for whom the Gospels were written. Above we established the fact that the Synoptic Gospels were written for the Jewish Christians, while the Gospel according to John was written for the Gentile Christians.[24] In the Synoptic Gospels which were written for the Jewish Christians, animosity was directed against the Pharisees to emphasize the fact that Jesus, although greatly influenced by the teachings of the Pharisees, and following their doctrines and beliefs, was rejected by them. In the Gospel according to John, which was written for Gentile Christians, animosity was directed against all the Jews.

The Gentile Christians had no interest in the Pharisees; many of them probably were entirely unaware of their existence. The hostility toward the Jews in this Gospel is intended to affirm the fact that Jesus, although by birth a Jew, was not accepted by his own people. With this clue, we can better understand why John does not mention any *halakic* disputes between Jesus and the Pharisees. They were of no interest to the Gentile Christians. The disputes between Jesus and the Pharisees were concentrated on the miracles of Jesus but not on the *Halakah*.

8. THE PHARISEES—SAVIORS OF JUDAISM

The Pharisees were not hypocrites; on the contrary, Pharisaism was the antithesis of hypocrisy. Judaism as we know it was formed by them; and no people could have survived if they were religiously such intolerable hypocrites as they are pictured in Matthew chapter 23. On the contrary, the Pharisees made it possible for Judaism to survive, despite the catastrophe that befell the Jewish people in the year 70 C.E. when the Temple was destroyed by the Romans, and the Jews were massacred in subsequent Hadrianic persecutions. They helped the Jews to keep Judaism alive during the dark period of the Middle Ages. Their spirit still helps them to overcome the humiliation and suffering heaped upon them in the ghettos created by Nazism.

The ideals and ideas which were developed by the Pharisees in that first century gave strength and courage to the Jews in the later centuries of their dispersion and wandering, privation and degradation. "To suffer and to hope" became the motto of the Jewish people. This motto did not arise fortuitously as a consequence of outer circumstances but was the result of spiritual integrity and idealism crystallized by the Pharisees

It is possible that, in the heat of the arguments between the disciples of Jesus and the Pharisees, the disciples accused the Pharisees of not accepting the doctrines of Jesus, and called them hypocrites for not stretching the law to suit the interests of the early Christians. Jesus, however, if he ever had any controversies with the Pharisees, did not call them hypocrites.

CHAPTER X

THE TRIAL AND THE CRUCIFIXION

HAVING described the complex and stormy background of the century that gave birth to the Christian Era, and having portrayed the clashing forces and interests —political, economic, social and religious—of that distant world, together with an analysis of the primary literary sources of the rise of Christianity, we are now in a position to understand better the climax of the Christian epic—the trial and crucifixion of Jesus.

It was only natural that the narrative of the Passion, as the story of the death of Jesus has come to be called, should have seized tremendous hold on the Christian imagination; indeed, many Christian scholars believe it was the first part of the Gospels to be committed to writing. For the trial and crucifixion of Jesus was the culmination and denouement of the whole dramatic struggle that gave birth to a new faith for mankind. This new faith wielded great influence not only on the life of its Christian devotees, but molded the whole course of human civilization.

1. THE STORY OF THE PASSION

The Passion narrative is recorded in the four Gospels. As mentioned previously, there is a fundamental discrepancy between the first three Gospels and the Fourth Gospel in so crucial a matter as the date of Jesus' crucifixion. It is not to be wondered at, then, that in the story of the trial and crucifixion the Synoptic Gospels are themselves replete with inconsistencies and obscurities. They are not even in accord in their portrayal of the events which took place from the time of the arrest of Jesus to his crucifixion.

The story of the Passion, as given in the Gospel of Mark, runs as follows:[1] The chief priests and the scribes sought to take Jesus by craft in order to destroy him. On the first day of the Feast of Unleavened Bread, when the Jews "killed the Passover" lamb, the disciples said to Jesus, "Where wilt thou that we go and prepare that thou mayest eat the Passover?" And while they were singing the hymns, Judas, one of the twelve disciples, came with a great multitude, armed with swords and staves, from the chief priests and the scribes and the elders.

Judas betrayed his Master, Jesus, with a kiss. Apparently, there was an understanding between him and the authorities that by the kiss he would signify the man, Jesus, for whom they were searching. Jesus complained against them for coming with swords and staves as if he were a *lestes* (a robber). Further, he declared that he was in the Temple teaching, and that they had no legal right to arrest him.

Jesus was led away to the house of the high priest where all the chief priests, the elders and the scribes had been assembled. Before the chief priests and all those gathered there, a Sanhedrin sought testimony against Jesus to put him to death; but they found none. Some men falsely witnessed against Jesus, asserting that he had declared that he would destroy the Temple that was made by human hands and would within three days build another not made by human hands.

However, the witnesses did not agree in their testimony. The high priest then arose and asked Jesus, "Art thou the Christ (Messiah), the Son of the Blessed?" And Jesus said, "I am and ye shall see the Son of Man sitting on the right hand of Power and coming in the clouds of heaven." The high priest, on hearing these words, rent his clothes and exclaimed, "What need we any further witnesses? Ye have heard the blasphemy."

The following morning the chief priests held a consultation with the elders and the scribes and the whole Sanhedrin. And Jesus was delivered to Pilate. When he was brought before the procurator, he was asked by Pilate, "Art thou the King of the Jews?" and he answered, "Thou sayest."

It was a fixed custom in those days to release a prisoner on festival days. Pilate, holding Jesus and another prisoner, asked the people whom he should release to them—Jesus, the King of the Jews, or Barabbas, a man who had committed murder during an insurrectionary episode. The chief priest had aroused the people to ask that Barabbas be granted freedom. Pilate granted their request, and Jesus, whom Pilate knew had been delivered to him because of the envy of the high priests, was led to be crucified.

They clothed Jesus with a purple robe and plaited a crown of thorns, and they saluted him, "Hail, King of the Jews!" When they had crucified him, they rented his garments, and they inscribed on the cross "The King of the Jews."

Two *lestai* (robbers) were also crucified with him, one to his right and one to his left side. When Jesus was on the cross, the chief priests and the scribes mocked and cried, "Let Christ, the King of Israel, descend now from the cross, that we may see and believe and they that were crucified with him also revile him." Thus, the Passion Story according to the Gospel of Mark.

2. DISCREPANCIES AND CONFUSIONS

The other Gospels reveal strange discrepancies as to the manner of the arrest of Jesus and his trial.

Gospel of Luke. Luke does not mention the fact that the elders were assembled in the house of the high priest when Jesus was arrested. He states that, after Jesus' arrest, in the morning "the elders of the people and the scribes came together and led him into their Sanhedrin,"[2] where they asked him if he was the Christ Messiah? He makes no mention of the high priest's accusation against Jesus of blasphemy. When Jesus was delivered to Pilate, the elders and scribes accused him of "perverting the nation and forbidding to give tribute to Caesar saying that he himself is Christ, a King."[3]

One of the two men who were crucified with Jesus reviled him and said, "if thou be Christ save thyself and us." However, the other malefactor told his comrade that he had unjustly reproached Jesus. "We," he said, "indeed justly suffer for we received the due reward of our deeds but this man hath done nothing amiss."[4]

Gospel of Matthew. In giving his account of the Passion, Matthew added a few episodes which are not found in the other two.

When Pilate was conducting the trial, his wife sent him an urgent warning. "Have thou nothing to do with that just man; for I have suffered many things this day in a dream because of him."[5]

Matthew recounts the incident that, when Pilate pronounced the sentence, he washed his hands before the people, and said, "I am innocent of the blood of this just man." To this the crowd replied, "His blood be on us and on our children."[6]

Gospel of John. John's account of the Passion[7] is in disagreement with the first three Gospels. He presents an entirely different picture of the trial of Jesus. The Gospel of John states that the chief priests and the Pharisees called a Sanhedrin and asked them what to do with Jesus who was performing miracles. They said to the Sanhedrin, "if we let him thus alone, all men will believe on him and the Romans shall come and take away both our place and our nation. And one of them named Caiaphas, being the high priest that same year, said unto them, 'You know nothing at all. Nor consider that it is expedient for us that one man should die for the people and that the whole nation perish not.' "[8]

John also relates how Judas betrayed his Master, Jesus. Judas, having received a cohort and officers from the chief priests and Pharisees, came to the place where Jesus was, with lanterns and torches and weapons. John does not mention the incident of the kiss by which Judas betrayed Jesus. The cohort and the captain and the officers of the Jews took Jesus and first led him to Annas who was the father-in-law of Caiaphas. This was the same Caiaphas, writes John, who advised the Jews that it was more beneficial that one man should perish for the Jews than that all the Jews should die for one man.

Later, Jesus was led to the judgment hall (Praeartium). The priests themselves did not enter the hall because, as the Gospel of John states, "Lest they should be defiled but that they might eat the 'Passover.'" Pilate, coming out, asked them what accusation they brought against Jesus. They answered that he was an evil-doer. That was why they were delivering Jesus to Pilate. Pilate, however, said to the accusers, "Take ye him and judge him according to your law." The Jews replied, "It is not lawful for us to put any man to death."

Then Pilate went into the judgment hall and called Jesus. He asked him, "Art thou the King of the Jews?" To this Jesus answered, "Sayest thou this thing of thyself, or did others tell it thee of me?"

John, like the Synoptic Gospels, relates that it was customary to release a prisoner for the Passover Festival. Pilate asked the Jews, "Shall I release unto you the King of the Jews?" The Jews in reply asked for the release of Barabbas who, according to John, was a *lestes*. (robber).

Pilate took Jesus and scourged him. Soldiers plaited a crown of thorns and put it upon his head and hailed him "King of the Jews." Pilate again came out and said to the Jews that he did not find any fault with him. However, the Jews cried out, "Crucify him!" Again Pilate repeated that he did not discover any fault in Jesus. The Jews answered him that according to their Law, he ought to die because he had proclaimed himself the "Son of God."

When Pilate heard this, he became frightened and entered again the judgment hall, and again examined Jesus. But Jesus gave him no answer. When Pilate said to Jesus, "I have power to crucify thee and have power to release thee," Jesus answered, "Thou couldst have no power at all against me except it were given thee from above. Therefore, he that delivered me unto thee had the greater sin."

John continues to relate that Pilate again wanted to release him but the Jews cried out and angrily asserted, "If thou let this man go, thou art not Caesar's friend." Pilate again asked the Jews, "Shall I crucify your king?" The chief priests answered, "We have no king but Caesar."

Pilate delivered Jesus to be crucified. He was crucified with two other men, one on each side. Pilate had inscribed the title to be put on the cross. The title read, "Jesus of Nazareth, the King of the Jews." These words were inscribed in Hebrew, Greek and Latin. The chief priests urged Pilate not to write the inscription "The King of the Jews" on the cross. Pilate answered, "What I have written, I have written." After he was crucified, the soldiers divided his garments in four parts among themselves.

Thus, the Gospels give a varied, confused and contradictory account of the arrest and the trial of Jesus.

The Arrest. According to the Synoptic Gospels, Jesus was arrested by a *multitude* who were sent by the high priests, the elders and the scribes. Then he was led to

Caiaphas, and there the high priests, the elders and the scribes were assembled and he was accused first of blasphemy. According to John, however, Jesus was arrested by a *cohort and officers* sent by the high priests and the Pharisees. The word "cohort" implies that the Roman authorities participated in his arrest. John tells further that he was first led to Annas, who was the father-in-law of Caiaphas, and from there he was brought to the high priest, Caiaphas. On the following morning, he was taken to the hall of judgment before Pilate. John's narration about the arrest is in direct contradiction to the account given in the Synoptic Gospels.

The Trial. There is no agreement, even in the Synoptic Gospels themselves, as to the manner of procedure at Jesus' trial.

According to Matthew and Mark, the scribes and elders were assembled in the house of the high priest, Caiaphas, and there Jesus was examined and indicted. According to Luke, Jesus was interrogated on the morning following his arrest when the elders, the high priests and the scribes assembled and brought him "into their Sanhedrin." Luke, however, does not mention that the high priest accused Jesus of blasphemy; Mark, on the other hand, does not record the crime which the high priest accused him of before Pilate. Luke does state that the accusation which the multitude brought against Jesus was that he perverted the nation, and forbade the people to pay tribute to Caesar by saying that he himself was "a Christ, a King."

Theory of emergency. The theory that Jesus' trial was a case of emergency is not sufficient to explain the suspension of all legalities. The emergency nature of the case is attributed to Jesus' popularity. The high priests feared that if Jesus had not been tried during Passover and put to death immediately, riots would have occurred in Jerusalem. We know, however, from the Gospels that Jesus, at the time of his arrest, was not popular with the great masses of the Jews.

When Pilate offered the Jews the release of Jesus, the Jews demanded his death—a clear indication that his popularity was not great among the rank and file of the people. As a matter of fact, there was no disturbance in Jerusalem during Passover, the time he was crucified, although many Jews from all over the country had assembled in Jerusalem. Neither can we assume that the trial was rushed through because Jesus had great influence with the authorities. He was as yet an obscure person and had had no dealings or influence with those in power.

According to the Gospel of John, the high priest said, "it is profitable for us that one man should die for the people and that the whole nation perish not." The question naturally arises why should the existence of the Jewish people be dependent upon the fate of Jesus?

The Charge of Blasphemy. When Jesus was arrested and brought before the high priest, he was asked, "Art thou the Christ, the Son of the Blessed?" To this Jesus answered, "I am and ye shall see the Son of Man sitting on the right hand of Power (God) and coming in the clouds of Heaven." When the high priest heard this, he rent his clothes and turned to the members of the assembly with these words, "Ye have heard the blasphemy. What think ye?" To this, the members of the assembly answered that Jesus was liable to death.

The word "blasphemy" is derived from the Greek and means slander, defamation, or, in general, abusive language. According to *Tannaitic* law, a man who uses abusive language against God cannot be put to death by a court.[9] At most he would be punished by divine visitation, that is, a person who uses slanderous language against God is liable to premature death, but that punishment rests in the hands of God. Only the man who cursed God with the name of God, "cursing God by the name of God,"[10] was liable to capital punishment. Jesus did not curse God.

Jesus' declaration that he would sit on "the right hand of Power (God)" cannot be considered blasphemy nor false prophecy. Many pious Jews looked forward to the future world where they would sit in the company of God and enjoy the Divine Glory.[11]

Jesus as rebel. When Jesus was brought before Pilate, the accusation made against him was that he was a rebel against the state, inciting the people not to pay tribute to Caesar, and asserting himself to be Christ, "The King of the Jews."

If the Sanhedrin convicted Jesus, they had the right to carry out the death sentence. As we have demonstrated in previous chapters, the Jews had the full right to do this. But John states that, when Pilate said to the Jews, "Take him and judge him according to your law," the Jews answered, "It is not lawful for us to put any man to death," which implies that they had no right to inflict capital punishment. It is indeed strange that the procurator had to be reminded by the Jews that the Romans had taken from them the right to inflict capital punishment.

Luke does not mention at all that the Sanhedrin convicted Jesus. If the Sanhedrin convicted Jesus for a religious crime, why did they have to bring him before Pilate at all, and accuse him? If we assume for the sake of argument that the Jews had no right to inflict capital punishment without ratification by the procurator, the procedure would have been simple—to present a report of the case to Pilate for ratification. Why then did they have to bring Jesus to Pilate in person? Such procedure would have been resorted to only where the defendant had a complaint to make to a higher court. The Gospels do not tell us that Jesus protested his conviction by the Sanhedrin.

Crucifixion as punishment. The very form of punishment that society inflicts upon those who break its laws is often characteristic of the society itself; so, too, in the case of the Jewish and Roman societies of the first century. We know that crucifixion was a Roman penalty and not a Jewish one. It was the most cruel and hideous of tortures, as Cicero said.[12] From the days of the Punic Wars, the Romans resorted to it as punishment for slaves. It was also applied by them to rebels. The procurator, Alexander Tiberus, crucified the two sons of Judas of Galilee.[13] Josephus relates that, after the capture of Jerusalem by Titus, he crucified so many Jews "there was not enough room for crosses nor enough crosses for the bodies." Josephus further states, "his (Titus) main reason for not stopping the crucifixions was the hope that the spectacle might perhaps induce the Jews to surrender, for fear that continued resistance would involve them in a similar fate."[14] The religious Sanhedrin had the right to inflict only four modes of capital punishment: stoning, burning, decapitation and strangling. But never did Jewish law permit crucifixion.

Questions. If Jesus was arrested for blasphemy or for any relgious offense, why did a Roman cohort come to arrest him? What had the Roman authorities to do with the arrest of a man who had committed a religious sin against Judaism? The Jews, it must be recalled, had religious autonomy.

What had the high priest to do with his arrest? The high priest held authority *only* over the Temple and its services, though he was also the political agent of the Roman authorities. The religious offender was under the jurisdiction of the religious Sanhedrin who had the full right to try, convict and punish such offender.

Again, why was Jesus brought to the house of the high priest? The ordinary procedure would have been to take him to the courthouse where the Sanhedrin tried their cases. We know that the Sanhedrin had their own special places where they held court. Why was it necessary to bring him to the house of the high priest, and assemble the Sanhedrin there? Jesus, according to the Gospels, was arrested in accordance with a plan laid several days before the act itself; hence, he should have been led straight to the courthouse. Moreover, was not

the session of the court illegal? We know that no Sanhedrin ever sat at night or on holydays to try cases.

Why then was Jesus crucified?

3. JESUS COMES TO JERUSALEM

The Jews were a vanquished people, crushed beneath
the heel of Roman imperialism. Crafty and cruel procurators ruled their land. The high priests were made
responsible to these procurators for the peace and tranquillity of the country. Many of the high priests thought
that, by appeasing the Romans and helping them to
destroy rebellious Jewish patriots, they would gain at
least temporary benefits for the Jews. They were what
we today call "appeasers." Some of the high priests,
however, sold themselves outright to the oppressors of
the Jews. They were comparable to the modern Quislings. Caiaphas most likely belonged to the second
group, the Quislings. That is the reason why Caiaphas
held the high priesthood for more than a decade. We
know that some of the high priests did not rule more
than a year. The fact that Caiaphas could hold this office
during the entire period of the procuratorship of Pilate
indicates that he was only a henchman carrying out the
whims of the crafty Pilate.

The high priests not only reported the activities of
the malcontented, but even arrested them. The Roman
cohort was at their disposal in seizing all suspicious
elements against the Roman state. When such a person
was arrested, he was first interrogated by the high priest
in the presence of his council (Sanhedrin). This council consisted of followers of the high priest who were

convened for this purpose. They did not have the right to try any culprit since the right to try a political offender had been taken away from them when Judea became a province of Rome. They only questioned the victim and presented his case before the procurator for trial. The procurator tried him and then either acquitted him (if that ever happened) or put him to death. He was scourged before he was executed. The death was by crucifixion.

Neither the procurators nor their hirelings, the high priests, succeeded in suppressing entirely Jewish resistance to Roman imperialism, nor in extinguishing the hope of the restoration of a free Judea under the scion of the family of David. Two groups were known at that time who particularly inflamed the people with the great desire and hope for freedom. They were the followers of the Fourth Philosophy and the Apocalyptists. Although their methods differed from each other, their goal was the same. The Roman authorities as well as their Jewish puppets regarded the members of these groups as a menace to the Jews, and these Jewish Quislings helped the Romans to destroy them.

Josephus relates a very interesting story which reflects the political conditions which prevailed in Judea during the time of the procurators.

A man by the name of Jesus, the son of Ananias, a farmer, standing in the Temple, suddenly began to cry out, "A voice against Jerusalem and the sanctuary . . . A voice against all the people." This Jesus went through the streets of Jerusalem day and night, crying out, "Woe to Jerusalem, woe to Jerusalem."

According to Josephus, this happened at the time when Albinus was the procurator, during the Festival of Tabernacles. Some of the leading men arrested this person and severely chastised him. However, in spite of his arrest and punishment, Jesus continued his cry, "Woe to Jerusalem." Then the leaders began to suspect the man to be under divine inspiration. Therefore, they turned him over to the procurator, Albinus. He was scourged, but the victim did not shed any tears, nor did he beg for mercy. When Albinus asked him why he uttered these cries, he never answered a word. Albinus in the end released him, taking him to be a mad man.[15]

As long as this man was considered merely a nuisance, disturbing the peace of the city, he was flogged by the authorities of Jerusalem. When, however, he was suspected of acting under divine influence, he was regarded as one of the Apocalyptists. The Jews had to turn him over to the procurator. Apocalyptists and persons suspected of being members of the Fourth Philosophy (the *Sicarii*)—being opposed to the Roman oppression—were considered rebels, and had to be delivered to the Roman rulers.

The fond expectation that a Jewish state would be re-established under a scion of David was warmly cherished by the Jewish masses. The Pharisees for centuries had preached to the Jews that God would restore their country under a Messiah of the House of David. From these hopes the common man in Israel drew strength and courage for dark days of oppression. Especially darkened were those days by the inner social strife which was sharp and bitter. Animosity prevailed between the *Ame Ha-aretz* (farmer folk) and the aristocracy; the Galilean farmers especially hated the high priests who compelled them to render tithes, sometimes forcibly.

Jesus, before entering the city of Jerusalem, was called by some people the Son of David. Upon arriving in Jerusalem, Jesus was hailed with these words, "Hosanna . . . blessed be the Kingdom of our father David that cometh in the name of the Lord."[16] He was also hailed, according to John, as the "King of Israel." "Hosanna, blessed is the King of Israel that cometh in the name of the Lord."[17]

According to the same Gospel, when Jesus was still in Galilee, some of his disciples wanted to make him King.[18] The acclamation of the people when Jesus entered Jerusalem as the "Son of David," "the King," was actually a rebellious act against the Jewish oppressors, the Romans. The proclamation of the Messiahship of Jesus and the affirmation that he was the Son of David, the King of Israel, was sufficient ground for the high priest to arrest Jesus. Had the high priest not suppressed such a movement, he would have been regarded by the Roman authorities as an accomplice in the insurrection.

Thus, the first stage of Jesus' entrance into Jerusalem was considered in the eyes of the "puppet" government a seditious act against Rome because of his being hailed as the Messiah.

Jews used to come to Jerusalem a few days before the Festival of Passover. Those days were tense in spirit.

Jews from all the four corners of the country flocked to the city. The governing gentry were jittery lest the people might be lured to revolt. The procurator who had his capital in Caesarea took up his residence in Jerusalem during the Passover Festival. He came to Jerusalem accompanied by armed forces. The change of residence of the procurator, and his display of force, revealed quite clearly how apprehensive the Romans were of overt acts of revolt during Passover.

The mere presence of the procurator in Jerusalem quickened the high priests, the Quislings, to become more alert to rumors or propaganda. They had to act swiftly to crush any agitation in embryo so that news of it should not reach the ear of the procurator. They were fearful of being suspected of having a share in disloyalty to Rome.

The first act recorded by the Gospels about Jesus' coming to Jerusalem was his going to the Temple. When Jesus entered the Temple, he drove out the money-changers from its midst. This act was a challenge against the authority of the high priest who ruled over the Temple precincts like a dictator. It was also a rebellious act against the social order in Judea, against the wealthy classes who were protected by the Romans.

It was not surprising, therefore, that Caiaphas, the high priest, as a representative of the interests of the Roman authorities, wanted to destroy Jesus. To make sure that Jesus was indeed a rebel against the Romans, Jesus was asked, "Is it lawful to give tribute to Caesar or not?" Jesus, recognizing the trap laid for him, answered with laconic and evasive words, "Render to

Caesar the things that are Caesar's, and to God the things that are God's."[19]

This answer was, to be sure, noncommittal. He did not say that the tribute should not be paid to Caesar and, hence, declare himself a rebel against the Romans. On the other hand, he did not assert that the tribute should be rendered to Caesar and, hence, expose disloyalty to the interests and ideals of the Jewish people.

4. TRIAL AND CRUCIFIXION—RECONSTRUCTED

As we attempt the historical reconstruction of the trial and crucifixion of Jesus, in the light of our preceding research, we must, first of all, divest our facts of their theological accent and, so far as possible, lay strong hold on the realities as we can discover them. Surprising as it may seem, if we keep close to historical facts, the contradictions and discrepancies, known to every student of the New Testament, will vanish. The Four Gospels, Synoptic and non-Synoptic, are not only dependent on each other but their narratives were based upon common traditions which were oral. Some inconsistencies in minor details were bound to occur. However, in regard to the essential substance of Jesus' arrest and its causes, as well as those who actually crucified him, they all agree.

On the night of Passover, while Jesus was eating the Paschal meal, the Last Supper, he was arrested.[20] His arrest was made possible through an act of betrayal. Judas, one of his twelve disciples, betrayed him. Judas came with a cohort and multitude of men from the high priests and the elders. Judas kissed Jesus. That was the sign given to the cohort that this man should be taken into custody; according to John, the kiss-sign was unnecessary. When Judas came with the cohort, Jesus asked, "Whom seek ye?" The cohort answered, "Jesus of Nazareth."

What caused Judas to betray his Master, Jesus? The Gospels give no answer to this query; they remain silent. Some believe that Judas may have been disappointed in his hope that Jesus would undertake the mission of Messianism. Others hold that Judas wished to compel Jesus to work miracles to save himself and thus to destroy the Roman oppressors of the Jews.[21] A readier conjecture, corroborated in the narrative, suggests itself.

Judas was a follower of the Apocalyptists and believed that Jesus was the *Son of God*. But Judas feared lest some disciples were ready that Passover night to declare Jesus the Messiah, the *King of the Jews*. He, therefore, went to the authorities and told them of these designs, and urged Jesus' arrest. He himself, as John records, led a Roman cohort to arrest Jesus. The cause of Judas' fear lay in the fact that, when Jesus entered Jerusalem, he was hailed as King of the Jews, the Son of David. Indeed, the question which was put to Jesus before Pilate was whether he was the Messiah, the King of the Jews; while on the cross were inscribed the words, "Jesus of Nazareth, King of the Jews."

We may add that the Gospel of John states that the disciples of Jesus wanted to make him king while Jesus was still in Galilee. Paul did not eliminate Judas from the twelve apostles. In his letter to the Corinthians, he still speaks of *twelve*.[22] It is indeed strange that Paul should still include Judas, the so-called betrayer, among the twelve. But we must not overlook the fact that Paul never regarded Jesus as the "King of the Jews." To Paul Jesus was the Son of God.

Jesus showed indignation at the time of his arrest. "Be ye come out as against a *lestes* (robber)?" he asked. Jesus was offended not because he was arrested, but because they came against him armed with swords. Jesus objected because they took him to be one of the followers of the Fourth Philosophy, who sought to effect their ideas by force, and were looked upon as "robbers," as they were designated by Josephus. Jesus, on the contrary, preached submission and even love toward the enemy, holding as his motto, "Whosoever shall smite thee on the right cheek turn to him the other also."

Jesus was then led into the house of the high priest who, as we know, was the political representative of the Jewish people for the Roman authorities. In his house, the high priest, the elders, the scribes and the entire Sanhedrin were assembled. This Sanhedrin, unlike the religious Sanhedrin, had no definite place to hold sessions; it had no statutory regulations, as the religious Sanhedrin had; it could be called to session any time of day or night, holyday or Sabbath.

This was undoubtedly a political Sanhedrin, and consisted of men who were called together by the high priest to determine the guilt of the accused. They were in truth merely the "rubber stamps" of the high priest. This was his Sanhedrin, as the Gospel of Luke states clearly, "And the scribes assembled and led him into *their* Sanhedrin." This assembly sought out witnesses against Jesus, but found none. Judas, who had betrayed Jesus, did not follow Jesus to the house of the high priest; therefore, there were no witnesses against Jesus.

The high priest asked Jesus, "Are you the Messiah Christ, the Son of the Blessed (Son of God)?" To this Jesus replied, "I am and ye shall see the Son of Man sitting on the right hand of Power (God)." When the high priest heard the words of Jesus, he tore his clothes and said that there was no need for witnesses since he had heard with his own ears abusive language against God. Thereupon, the entire assembly thought such a man was liable to the death penalty.

Apparently, the high priest so presented the case to his Sanhedrin that Jesus, who claimed to be the Messiah, the "King of the Jews," should be delivered up to the Romans. Jesus was not held to be so important and worthy that, on account of him, an entire people should be destroyed, since he was regarded as a sinner who used abusive language against God. John put this more definitely when he wrote that the high priest said that Jesus should be delivered to the Romans since he was hailed to be the "King of the Jews," and hence many Jews would follow him. This might have given occasion for the Romans to suspect that the Jews were planning to revolt. In retaliation, the Romans might have destroyed the entire Jewish nation.

On the morrow morning, according to Mark and Matthew, the high priest and the elders and the scribes and all the Sanhedrin held a council, and they delivered Jesus to Pilate. Luke, however, records only one session of the Sanhedrin, that of the morning. Apparently, there had to be a continuous session the whole night after Jesus' arrest, since they could not bring Jesus before Pilate in the middle of the night, and they had to wait for morning. (The first two Gospels relate in detail what happened after the arrest up to the time when Jesus came before Pilate, while Luke gives only the general story without details. Hence, there are no contradictions among the Synoptists. John, written only for Gentile Christians, was interested only in telling of the arrest of Jesus, its cause, and the trial before Pilate. What happened to Jesus when he was brought to the house of Caiaphas, the high priest, was for John merely an incidental episode, unimportant for Gentile Christian readers.)

In establishing that the Sanhedrin which was assembled in the house of Caiaphas was not a religious Sanhedrin but was a political Sanhedrin, we remove automatically all the apparent discrepancies and illegalities in connection with the trial of Jesus. Note that the first query put to Jesus by Pilate was whether he was the "King of the Jews." To this Jesus answered, "Thou sayest." This laconic answer was evasive. He neither denied nor affirmed this accusation against him. Luke adds that, when Jesus was brought before Pilate, the Jews accused him of forbidding them to pay tribute to Caesar, "saying that he himself is Christ (Messiah) a King." To this Pilate inquired whether he was truly the "King of the Jews." Thus, it is quite clear that Jesus was arrested and brought before Pilate as *a political offender against the Roman state.* The accusation made against him was that he claimed himself to be the King of the Jews.

When Jesus was brought before Pilate, John states, Pilate asked the priests what was the charge against Jesus. They answered that Jesus was an evildoer. Pilate, observing Jesus closely, saw that this man could not be a source of great danger to the Roman state. Pilate thought that the accusation against Jesus was of a religious character. Therefore, he turned to the high priest and said, "Take ye him and judge him according to your law."

The Jews replied that Jesus was a political offender and hence, they declined to try a political offender; such a person should be turned over to the procurator. It is quite possible that the high priest did not want to accept Pilate's offer to try Jesus for a religious offense, because the high priest feared that Pilate was playing politics with him. He was apprehensive lest, if the Jews should convict Jesus, they would be accused of convicting a man of a political crime, something which they had no legal right to do. On the other hand, if they were to acquit Jesus, they would be accused of releasing a political offender against the Romans. We know from Philo and Josephus the treacherous nature of Pontius Pilate.

Pilate according to the Gospels sought to take advantage of the custom prevalent in Judea,[23] of releasing a prisoner for the Passover Festival. He asked the Jews whether they wanted Barabbas to be released or Jesus, the King of the Jews. Barabbas, according to Mark, had been imprisoned for participating in a revolt. He

was a political offender. Under pressure of the high
priest, the people asked for the freedom of Barabbas.
(According to John the people asked for the freedom of
Barabbas without the pressure of the high priest.) Apparently, Barabbas was a member of the Fourth Philosophy who, we know, caused many revolts against the
Romans and killed many people, not only Romans but
also those who submitted to the Romans.

Pontius Pilate, according to Mark and John, when
he offered to release Jesus to the Jews, called him dis-
tinctly the "King of the Jews." The high priest, therefore, had sufficient reason to fear a trap, lest Pilate
might accuse him later of having had a share in the
conspiracy against the Roman state by accepting Jesus
as "King of the Jews." As a matter of fact, when Pilate
later asked the Jews, "Shall I crucify your King," the
chief priests protested, "We have no king but Caesar."
Note that Pilate did not say, "Shall I crucify Jesus,"
but "the King." The fact that the high priest had to
assert again and again, "We have no king but Caesar,"
indicates that not only was Jesus' trial a political issue
but that the high priest was fearful of being accused
of being an accomplice in declaring Jesus a King of the
Jews.

The apprehension of the high priests was very strong.
They were fearful that Pilate was scheming to involve
them as accomplices of Jesus in his claim to be the King
of the Jews. When Pilate, according to John, wrote the
titulus (the Roman method, as we learn from Suetonius,[24] of publishing the reason for the execution on
the cross), the "King of the Jews," the high priest asked

him not to write, "The King of the Jews but that he (Jesus) said 'I am the King of the Jews.'" The high priests feared the inscription on the cross, "Jesus, the King of the Jews," because Pilate might use it as a weapon against them.

Not all the Jews who were present at the trial were anxious that Jesus be condemned and put to death. When Jesus was led to be crucified, Luke tells us, "There followed him a great company of people and of women which also bewailed and lamented him."[25] Many Jews were sorely distressed on seeing Jesus led to death.

Pilate, John relates, came out a number of times from the judgment hall to argue with the Jews and to tell them that he did not find Jesus guilty of any crime. To this the Jews answered, "We have a law and by our law he ought to die because he made himself the Son of God." But, there is no Jewish law, either in the Bible or in the *Talmud* to the effect that a person who claims to be the "Son of God" is liable to capital punishment. The use of the expression "Son of God" was common among the Apocalyptists. In the Book of *Enoch* the expression is found, "And I and My Son."[26] In the Psalms we also find the expression "My Son" in the words of God, which most likely referred to David.[27] When John uses the word "law," he does not refer to the Jewish law but the law of Caesar. As a matter of fact, some manuscripts omit the word "our" and, hence, he undoubtedly refers to the law of the Romans. Jesus' reference to himself as Messiah and the "Son of God" was tantamount to challenging the authority of Caesar over the Jews.

The Jews did not enter the judgment hall that night, on account of eating the Paschal Lamb. Therefore, Pilate, in order to speak to them, had to come out from the judgment hall.[28]

Jesus was condemned by Pilate, and was crucified. On his cross, as has been stated, were inscribed the words, "Jesus of Nazareth, King of the Jews." From the penalty which Jesus suffered, namely, crucifixion, and from the *titulus*, it is clear that Jesus was put to death for the political offense of claiming to be the King of the Jews.

Jesus was crucified between two *lestai* (robbers). The King James version reads "thieves." This translation is incorrect.[28a] The word, "thief" in the Gospels is rendered in Greek by the word *kleptes*.[29] The men who were crucified with Jesus were probably members of the Fourth Philosophy who were usually called *lestai* (robbers). When Jesus was crucified, the soldiers confiscated his garments.[30] This confirms the opinion that Jesus was put to death as a political offender, for in the case of anyone put to death by the religious Sanhedrin, his property belonged to his heirs; but anyone put to death for political reasons, lost his property to the state.

The mockery to which Jesus was subjected strangely reveals the zeal of the high priests to dissociate themselves from Jesus. Jesus was reviled by the soldiers mocking him with the words, according to Luke, "If thou be the King of the Jews, save thyself." The high priests and the scribes also, according to the Gospels, reviled Jesus; Mark and Matthew narrate that they taunted him, "Let Christ the King of Israel descend now from the cross that we may see and believe."[31] Jesus, throughout the Passion, was called the King of the Jews. Upon his arrival in Jerusalem, he was hailed by the same title. When he was reviled by the soldiers, he was called the King of the Jews. However, when the high priests reviled him, they did not use the phrase the "King of the Jews," but "King of Israel."

What was the reason for this different title? Certainly, it cannot be laid to a slip of a scribe's pen, nor a verbal error in the oral tradition of the Synoptic Gospels. There must have been some genuine distinction underlying it. Now, the people who lived in the country of Judea were called Judeans, *Jews,* while their coreligionists in the Diaspora outside of Judea were called not Judeans, but *Israelites.*[32] Theological differences were involved in this differing terminology. Hence, when the high priests, fearful of being accused of sympathy with the followers of Jesus—rebels against the Romans, and establishers of an independent Judea—reviled Jesus, they did not dare even in mockery to call him the King of the Jews.

That the religious Sanhedrin had nothing to do with the trial of Jesus may be deduced from the fact that, though the first three Gospels—especially in the controversies between the Pharisees and the disciples of Jesus—exhibit great hostility toward the Pharisees, yet at the trial of Jesus the Pharisees were in no way implicated. It is obvious that if Jesus had been tried by the religious Sanhedrin, the first three Gospels would not have failed to attack the Pharisees, since we know that the religious Sanhedrin was dominated by the Pharisees.

The Fourth Gospel, John, does not show any animosity toward the Pharisees, but for another reason. Hostility in this Gospel is directed against the *Jews as a whole*. As we have many times stated, the Gospel according to John was written for Gentile Christians, and the Gentiles had no interest in the Pharisees; indeed, many of them probably were entirely unaware of their existence. The hostility toward the Jews in this Gospel was intended to emphasize the fact that Jesus, although by birth a Jew, was not accepted by his own people, and that the destruction of the Temple was a punishment for their rejection of Jesus.

John's evident purpose, as we shall show in due course, was to blame the Jewish people for the arrest of Jesus and his delivery to Pilate for trial. For this reason chiefly, he connected the Pharisees with the arrest of Jesus since they and the high priests represented the people, the former in religious and the latter in political affairs.

5. THE JEWS DID NOT CRUCIFY JESUS

A superficial reading of the story of the Passion gives the impression that the Jews were responsible for the crucifixion of Jesus. As we analyzed the narrative of the trial and crucifixion against the background of the times, however, it became evident that the Jewish people were not responsible for the death of Jesus.

Jesus was crucified as the King of the Jews. The Jewish religious Sanhedrin and the Jewish people had nothing to do with the trial of Jesus. The high priest who actually delivered Jesus to the Roman authorities either was compelled to do so to save himself so as not to be accused of being an accessory to the rebels; or, most likely, Caiaphas, the high priest, played the rôle of a Quisling who proved ready to sell out Judea to the Romans for personal gain.

The Jewish people were crushed under Roman tyranny. The Roman authorities punished not only the individuals who incited the people against the Romans, but the leaders of the people as well. The Jewish leaders, we may say, were held as hostages for the submission of the Jewish people to the Roman state. Many Jewish leaders in such circumstances and political conditions had to act as informers against the dissenters and revolutionaries among their brethren in order to save their own lives. Some of them, as we have already pointed out, sold themselves entirely to the Roman authorities for their own benefit, as may have been the case of the high priest, Caiaphas.

Our own times make such political duplicities all too real to us. In countries conquered and overrun by the Nazis, some of the leaders of the conquered people are compelled to inform the German authorities of those who plot against the tyranny of the Nazis; some of them, as is well known to everyone, sold themselves to the Germans and betrayed their own people—the Quislings.

The Synoptic Gospels, as a matter of fact, do not ascribe the death of Jesus to the Jews. Mark 10:33 reads, "And the Son of Man shall be delivered unto the chief priests and unto the scribes and they shall condemn him to death and they shall deliver him to the Gentiles." (The same passage is found in Matthew 20:18.) Some manuscripts, however, omit the word "death." In that case the gravamen of the charge against the high priests and their leaders would be that they condemned him and delivered him to the Gentiles, but not that the Jewish leaders put Jesus to death. It is impossible to believe that, if the word "death" had been in the primitive Mark and Matthew, a copyist would have omitted this word. During the Middle Ages the Church preached that the Jews crucified Jesus. Therefore, no copyist would have dared omit the word "death." However, if the primitive Matthew and Luke did not have the word "death," some later copyist, under the influence of church teaching, inserted the word "death" in its present place.

The Synoptic Gospels accused the Jews only of rejecting Jesus, but they did not accuse them of his death. This is quite evident from another passage, Mark 8:31, "And he (Jesus) began to teach them that the Son of Man must suffer many things and be rejected of the elders and of the chief priests and scribes and be killed and after three days rise again." Here the accusation brought against the priests and the elders is that *they rejected him* but not that they put him to death. And this is confirmed by the other two Synoptists.

It is true that the Gospel according to John laid the blame for the crucifixion upon the Jews. But we must again be reminded that this Gospel was written more than a few decades after the destruction of the Temple.

Some New Testament scholars even place this Gospel at the end of the first quarter of the second century.

The animosity between the Jews and the new sect, the Christians, had by then become very intense. Nor should we forget that this Gospel was written for Gentiles. The evangelist wanted to convey the idea to the Gentiles that the Jews, who rejected the Gospel, had killed the Master; but, that the Roman procurator who had sent Jesus to his execution was convinced of his innocence. The early Christians sought to ingratiate themselves with the Roman authorities so that they should not look upon a Roman convert to Christianity as one who would side with the Jews, the rebels. In the great war (65-70 c.e.) between the Jews and the Romans, the Christians of Jerusalem left the city for Pella in order that they might not have to take part in the war against the Romans. Since the policy of the early Christians was not to antagonize the Romans, they tried to put the blame for the crucifixion upon the Jews.

The Gospel according to Matthew tells us that, when Pilate condemned Jesus, he washed his hands as a symbol of his innocence and said, "I am innocent of the blood of this just person." Washing the hands as a symbol of innocence was not known to the Romans. It was practiced among the ancient Jews. It is paradoxical that Pilate, whom Philo pictures as one of the most cruel persons who murdered even innocent people without any trial, became of a sudden a man of scruple and of conscience, and did not want to put Jesus to death.

These verses, undoubtedly, are a later edition to show

that the Jews, not Pilate, were responsible for his crucifixion. When the Christians strove to exonerate the
Romans from this guilt, they placed the responsibility
for the crucifixion upon the Jews. And hence, the entire story was inserted as if put into the mouth of the
Jews, "his blood be on us, and on our children." If
anyone had the right to wash his hands when Pilate
crucified Jesus, certainly the Jewish people had that
right, for they were blameless of the death of Jesus. It
is noteworthy that no other Gospel mentioned this
incident.

The question may arise: if Pilate was so cruel and
unscrupulous, why did he remain so long in Judea as
procurator? Why was he not dismissed by Tiberius
Caesar? This is readily explained by the fact that the
real ruler in Rome was a man named Sejanus. This
Sejanus was a most unscrupulous person who, by treachery and craft, killed not only Romans but the son of
Caesar himself.[33] According to Philo,[34] he hated the
Jews and schemed to destroy them. The appointment
of Pilate came most likely from Sejanus himself, and
hence, Pilate went on with his cruelty against the Jews,
knowing that he would be protected by the ruler of
Rome, Sejanus.

The story of the Passion as given in Matthew is undoubtedly colored by some prejudice against the Jews.
Therefore, to balance the attitude of Matthew, as well
as the other two Synoptists, other passages not directly
in the narration of the Passion—and there are a number of such references—ought to be utilized. From these

passages an impartial opinion can be derived as to whom the Synoptists considered guilty of the death of Jesus.

When Jesus was still in Galilee, Matthew relates, he said to the disciples, "that he (Jesus) must go unto Jerusalem and suffer many things and be rejected by the elders and chief priests and scribes and be killed and be raised again the third day."[35] This Gospel, as well as the other two Synoptists[36] who have this story, accuse the chief priests *not* of putting Jesus to death, but merely of rejecting him.

That the Jews had a share in the guilt of the crucifixion of Jesus, the reader of the Passion story may be erroneously convinced on a surface reading of the Synoptic Gospels. However, on examining the readings of the manuscripts such a conclusion is not justifiable. Matthew 23:34, the Revised Version reads, "Wherefore, behold, I send unto you prophets and wise men and scribes and some of them ye shall kill and crucify and some of them shall ye scourge in your synagogues." The words, "and crucify and some of them ye will scourge in your synagogues," are omitted from some of the manuscripts, which indicates that they were not in the original Matthew.

Matthew 26:4 states, "And they consulted that they might take Jesus by subtility and kill him." The same story is recorded in Mark.[37] However, some manuscripts of this passage of Matthew do not contain the words "and kill him"; but some manuscripts of Mark do not contain the words "by subtility."

Matthew 27:1 relates, "When the morning was come all the chief priests and elders of the people took coun-

sel to put him to death." However, according to the
reading of some manuscripts, these words should read
"in order that he might be condemned to death." That
indicates only that the high priest and the elders, the
members of the political Sanhedrin, turned Jesus over
to Pilate for trial which ultimately led to his death. It
must be noted that this passage is not recorded in Mark
or Luke. They tell of the delivery of Jesus by the high
priest and the elders to Pilate but the words "to put
him to death" are not found there.

Luke tells a story that, after Jesus was crucified, two
men were walking from Jerusalem and were conversing
with each other. Jesus joined them, but the men did
not recognize him. Jesus asked them what they were
talking about. One of them answered that they were
conversing about Jesus of Nazareth and "How the chief
priests and (our) the rulers delivered him to the Court
to be condemned to death and to be crucified."[38] Again,
this passage in Luke accused the priest and the elders
at most of *delivering Jesus to Pilate for judgment.*

Neither Peter nor Paul accused the Jews of crucifying Jesus. They accused the Jews only of delivering
Jesus to Pilate. Peter said to the Jews, according to the
Book of Acts, "Whom ye delivered up to the court and
denied him in the presence of Pilate when he decided
to release him."[39] When Peter stood before the Sanhedrin and the high priest, he told them, "The God of
our fathers raised up Jesus whom ye slew and hanged
on the tree."[40] However, the Greek word *diecheirisasthe*
may be rendered as "procuring someone's death."

Hence, Peter accused the high priest of causing Jesus' death.

Paul, in his first Epistle to the Corinthians, speaks of the crucifixion of Jesus by "the princes of this world."[41] By this Paul meant that the early authorities were responsible for Jesus' crucifixion. The early authorities of the time of the crucifixion were the Romans. In his first Epistle to the Thessalonians, Paul used the expression, "Who both killed the Lord Jesus."[42] However, this phrase cannot be taken literally, as is quite evident from the text itself. For Paul says the following in the same epistle, "Who both killed the Lord Jesus and their own prophets and have persecuted us; and they please not God, and are contrary to all men, forbidding us to speak to the Gentiles that they might be saved."

Paul evidently had in mind the moral responsibility of the Jews for the crucifixion of Jesus. He could not have meant that the Jews actually prohibited him from speaking to the Gentiles. The Jews had no authority to do this in the Diaspora. He meant the Jews were responsible for this; they prevented him from preaching to the Gentiles. Similarly, must the phrase "killed the Lord Jesus" be interpreted, namely, that the Jews procured the death of Jesus by delivering him to Pilate. Furthermore, Paul could not accuse the Jews of killing Jesus since crucifixion, as we have pointed out, was not a Jewish form of execution. Both Peter and Paul accused the leaders of the Jews (the puppet authorities of Judea) at most of delivering Jesus to the court of Pilate.

The Apostolic Fathers never accused the Jews of the crucifixion of Jesus. In their polemics against Judaism —which were many—they never once used this accusation. What the Apostolic Fathers did charge the Jews with was their delivering Jesus to Pilate. The Apostolic Father, Ignatius, in his Epistle to the Trallians, said, "Who (Jesus Christ) was of the family of David and Mary who was truly born, both ate and drank, was truly persecuted under Pontius Pilate."

Likewise, Tacitus, the pagan historian, confirmed the fact that Pilate put Jesus to death. "Christus, the founder of the name, had undergone the death penalty in the reign of Tiberius, by sentence of the procurator, Pontius Pilate."[43]

We have thus proved that the crucifixion of Jesus was committed by Pilate, the Roman procurator, not by the Jews. True, the high priest delivered Jesus to Pilate for trial but that was not done by the will of the *Jewish people*. Political conditions which prevailed at that time in Judea forced some of the leaders to fight against their own brethren, and to help the Romans to destroy the real Jewish patriots.

The Jewish people did not crucify Jesus.

This charge was conceived in a later period, and was introduced into the records of the past. Hence, this accusation against the Jews, so fraught with misery, suffering and death, is a tragic libel evilly wrought on an innocent people.

The Synoptic Gospels, Peter and Paul, and the Apostolic Fathers—in a word, the founders of Christianity, and the creators of the Church—have never accused the Jewish people of the death of Jesus of Nazareth.

CHAPTER XI

PETER AND STEPHEN BEFORE THE SANHEDRIN

PETER and Paul, after Jesus, were two of the greatest figures in early Christianity. Peter whose name was Simon was one of the Twelve Apostles. Paul whose Hebrew name was Saul was the Apostle to the Gentiles, the real spiritual creator of Christianity.

The following chapters will demonstrate that Peter and Paul were tried by a political Sanhedrin for a political offense against the Romans in the same manner as Jesus; and they, like Jesus, were executed by the Romans. The question now arises: Why were they tried by a Sanhedrin? What sin had they committed against the Jews and Judaism that they should be so tried?

Jesus was born a Jew and died a Jew. Throughout his entire ministry, he preached his doctrines and ideas to no people other than his own, the Jewish.[2] It was only after his death, when his disciples maintained that Jesus was resurrected, that a new religious group began to develop. Some of his disciples, particularly Paul, spread the new religion among the pagans. For the first two decades after the crucifixion, the Jewish, as well as the Roman authorities, looked upon this group as being political, since they were the followers of Jesus who had been acclaimed as the King of the Jews. In due time this group lost its political aspect and became religious, and it was later persecuted by the Romans as a religious sect which sought to destroy Roman society and state.

1. THE TRIAL OF PETER

The source for the trials of Peter, Paul and Stephen is The Acts. Unlike the trial of Jesus for which we have the Four Gospels, the trials of Peter and Paul are preserved only in one source—The Acts. Like the Gospels, the Book of Acts is filled with theological ideas, for the author had a message to give to the early Christians.

An impartial account of these trials is more difficult for the historian because he has only one source upon which to draw. The difficulty increases because of the impossibility of verifying the authenticity of the records as was the case in the trial of Jesus. However, a careful scrutiny of the various manuscripts with the added help of knowledge of the background of the time will enable us to reach a truer picture of what transpired. No event is isolated, but is an integral part of other events as effect or cause, and is connected with other personalities. Hence, an historian must consult contemporary sources which may illuminate events and personalities associated with his main interest. Therefore, in the trials of Peter and Paul we must turn to the books of Josephus and to contemporary Roman writers. They will supply additional data to what we already know from the main source—The Acts.

The Book is divided into two parts—the activities of Peter, the Apostle to the Jews, and the activities of Paul, the Apostle to the Gentiles.

From The Acts we learn that when Peter was in the Temple he preached about the resurrection of Jesus. The priests and the captain of the Temple and the

Sadducees put him in custody "until the next day for it was now eventide." On the next day the rulers and the scribes assembled in Jerusalem. Peter was brought to the assembly. He was asked, "By what power or by what name have ye done this? Then Peter filled with the Holy Ghost said to them, 'Ye rulers of the people and leaders . . . be it known to you all and to all the people of Israel that by the name of Jesus Christ of Nazareth whom ye crucified whom God raised from the dead,' even by him doth this man stand here before all you."

Then the high priest and all who were with him, the Sadducees, arrested Peter; they put him in a public ward. On the following morning the high priest summoned the Sanhedrin and all the elders of "the children of Israel" and dispatched men to bring Peter from the jail. When Peter stood before the Sanhedrin, the high priest questioned him saying, "Did not we straitly commend you that ye should not teach in this name and, behold ye have filled Jerusalem with your doctrine and intend to bring this man's blood upon us." To this Peter answered that he ought to obey God rather than man, the God who raised Jesus whose death was procured and who was hanged on the tree, "him had God exalted with his right hand, and to be prince (ruler) and a saviour."[3]

Before analyzing this account of the arrest of Peter one statement of his must be clarified. We refer to the words of Peter "whom ye crucified." Apparently, the author of The Acts put in the mouth of Peter the accusation that the Jews crucified Jesus. This accusation of Peter contradicts the other passage in The Acts where Peter accused the Jews only of delivering Jesus "to the court and denied him in the presence of Pilate."[4] These two utterances are in disagreement. The saying that the Jews crucified Jesus was a favorite expression used by the writer of The Acts to accuse the Jews of persecuting the early Christians. The author quotes another statement of Peter using the words "this Jesus whom ye crucified." It is needless to repeat again that the expression "ye crucified" could not be applied to the Jews. All the Four Gospels agree that Jesus was crucified by the order of Pilate and the Roman soldiers nailed him on the cross. Therefore, it is quite evident that the expression "ye crucified Jesus" could not be applied to the Jews.

We must not forget that the early Christian tradition was that Luke who wrote his Gospel was also the author of The Acts.[5] In the Gospel of Luke as was said, the accusation against the chief priests and the rulers was that they "delivered him to the court to be condemned to death and to crucify him."[6] Thus, the accusation of Luke was that the chief priests and the leaders of the Jews had delivered Jesus to Pilate and therefore, they carried only the moral responsibility for the act. The author of The Acts (Luke), however, considered the moral responsibility for the crucifixion to imply that the chief priests and the rulers themselves had performed the act.

In due course, we shall show that the Book of The Acts was written not earlier than the end of the first century and in the Diaspora. We must not overlook the fact that when The Acts was written the Christians tried to justify Christianity in the eyes of the Romans. Hence, it was necessary for them not to mention the fact that Jesus was crucified by the Romans.

From the account given in The Acts of the arrest of Peter, we may readily see that the chief priests, the captain of the Temple, and the Sadducees arrested Peter for teaching that Jesus arose after his death and was made by God the *ruler* of the Jews. Peter could not have been tried before a religious Sanhedrin. He did not commit any religious offense, since maintaining that Jesus was resurrected could not have been considered such.

The idea of resurrection was a much disputed subject among the Jews. The Sadducees denied any resurrection. The Pharisees, however, believed in it. No one, as far as we know, was ever held in jail or tried by the Pharisees for disbelief in resurrection. Peter could only have been tried for associating himself with Jesus who claimed to be the King of the Jews. Therefore, we can very well understand that the high priest did not summon Peter to stand trial before the Sanhedrin; the Book of Acts relates that the high priest assembled a Sanhedrin which would indicate that it was a political Sanhedrin since such a Sanhedrin had to be summoned to try offenders against the state. The religious Sanhedrin would not have to be summoned since it had its permanent place where it held court.

As in the trial of Jesus, who was accused of a political offense and was tried by the political Sanhedrin, so we learn that Peter was likewise tried by a political Sanhedrin for a political offense. Again, as in the arrest of Jesus, the high priest who actually delivered Jesus to the Roman authorities was compelled to do so in order not to be accused of being an accessory to the rebels. So, in the trial of Peter, the same motive as in the trial of Jesus caused the arrest of Peter.

From the narrative given in The Acts about the arrest and trial of Peter, we may infer that the rulers of the Jews who were held responsible to the Roman authorities for the tranquillity of Judea, were more concerned with Peter's teachings that Jesus the Messiah Christ had arisen from death and was exalted by God as the ruler of the Jews. The Jewish leaders were fearful that the Romans would accuse them of encouraging an insurrection against the Roman state. From The Acts we learn further that on the day after Peter's arrest, the rulers and the elders and the scribes assembled, and had Peter brought before them and questioned in whose name was he announcing the fulfillment of the actual resurrection. The answer was given them by Peter that he was doing so in the name of Jesus of Nazareth the Messiah Christ whom God had raised from the dead.

The Book of Acts continues to relate that the elders and the high priests prohibited Peter from teaching in the name of Jesus. Peter, nevertheless, continued his teachings. The high priest and his followers who belonged to the sect of the Sadducees arrested him and ordered him held in the detention house. The Sad-

ducees were particularly antagonistic to Peter for teach
ing the doctrine of resurrection which they strongly
opposed. The following morning the high priest and
those with him summoned the Sanhedrin and all the
elders (of the children of Israel).[7] Peter was brought
from the detention house to answer the accusations
charged against him before the Sanhedrin.

The high priest questioned Peter as to why he continued to teach against his orders and wished to bring
upon the Jews "the blood of this man (Jesus)." This is
a direct contradiction to the words of Matthew where,
according to his Gospel, the Jews said to Pilate, "his
blood be on us and on our children." According to
The Acts, however, the high priest said to Peter that
by his teachings he wished to bring upon the Jews the
blood of Jesus. From which it may be inferred that the
Jews denied responsibility for Jesus' death.

However, this statement "and wish to bring on us
the blood of this man" may have an entirely different
meaning. The high priest told Peter that his teachings
that Jesus arose from the dead and that he was the
ruler of the Jews might bring them into trouble with
the Roman government. The Roman government
would hold them as accomplices in the activities of
Jesus, who was crucified by them as the King of the
Jews. That may be the meaning of the words "and
wish to bring on us the blood of this man"; namely,
the responsibility of the activities of the man whom
they put to death.

To the injunction that he should not teach in the
name of Jesus, Peter replied that he was compelled

to obey God rather than men, since Jesus was exalted by God to be the Ruler and the Saviour of the Jews. Peter's utterances offended the members of the Sanhedrin and they deliberated whether he and the apostles should be put to death. According to the same source, a man by the name of Gamaliel, a Pharisee, a scholar honored by all the people, appealed to the members of the assembly with the following words: "Men of Israel, take heed to yourselves with regard to these men what you are going to do." He reminded them that in previous years two other men, Theudas and Judas the Galilean, had stirred up some of the people to revolt against the Romans; and that both perished. Gamaliel continued to appeal to the members of the assembly: "Keep away from these men and let them alone, for if this plan or this work be of men, it will be destroyed; but if it be of God, you cannot destroy it then, lest you be found to be fighting even against God."[8]

From Gamaliel's remarks we may say that Peter was summoned before the Sanhedrin as a political offender and not for a religious crime. For Theudas and Judas the Galilean, whom Gamaliel mentioned, had led insurrections against the Roman authorities. The activities of Theudas are described by Josephus in the following passage: "Now while Fadus was procurator of Judea, a sorcerer named Theudas persuaded a great crowd to take their possessions and follow him to the River Jordan, for he said that he was a prophet from God and that he could dry the river by his command and give them an easy passage across it. By saying this, he deceived many. Fadus, however, did not allow them to enjoy their madness but sent out a squadron of cavalry against them which made an unexpected attack. He killed many and took many alive, but when they captured Theudas himself, they cut off his head and took it to Jerusalem."[9] As to the activities of Judas the Galilean, Josephus writes, "A Galilean named Judas incited his countrymen to revolt, upbraiding them as cowards for consenting to pay tribute to the Romans and tolerating mortal masters, after having God for their lord."[10]

Thus, from Josephus we learn that Theudas and Judas the Galilean, both incited the people to rebel against the Roman authorities. Gamaliel, in his address before the assembly, compared Peter's activities with those of these two men, who were political rebels and who had instigated the Jews against the Romans. He did not compare Peter's teachings with those of any false prophets who tried to beguile the Jews and change the laws handed down by Moses. The speech of Gamaliel had its effect upon the leaders, and they dismissed Peter, after they reproved him and prohibited him from preaching in the name of Jesus. Later, however, Peter was again arrested and brought to trial before Herod Agrippa.

2. THE TRIAL OF STEPHEN

In due time the followers of Jesus became a religious group. The political aspect of Jesus, as a Messiah who claimed to be the King of the Jews, became less conspicuous. The Jews looked upon these followers as heretics, who, in the name of Jesus, sought to abrogate the precepts of the Torah.

The Book of Acts describes the trial of Stephen as follows:

Then they prompted some men who said, "We have heard him speak blasphemous words against Moses and God." And they aroused the people and the elders and the scribes, and they fell upon him and seized him and brought him to the Sanhedrin, and they stood up false witnesses saying, "This man does not cease speaking words against this holy place and the Law. For we have heard him say that this Jesus, the Nazarene, will destroy this place and change the customs which Moses handed down to us" . . . And when they heard this they were deeply wounded, and they gnashed their teeth at him. But being full of the Holy Spirit he looked up to the sky and saw the glory of God and Jesus standing on the right hand of God, and said, "Behold I see the skies open and the Son of man standing on the right hand of God." And they cried out with a loud voice, and shut their ears, and rushed together against him, and threw him out of the city and began to stone him.[11]

The trial of Stephen, in contrast to that of Peter, was purely for a religious offense. The charge against him was that he spoke words of blasphemy (abusive language) against God and Moses, and for this he was brought before the Sanhedrin. The witnesses who testified before the Sanhedrin against him maintained that they heard him say that Jesus the Nazarene changed the laws and customs which Moses handed down to the people. This was a purely religious accusation. Unlike the trial of Peter, where the high priest summoned a Sanhedrin to try him, in the trial of Stephen, he was arrested and was brought before a sitting Sanhedrin. The reason for such a difference of procedure was due to the fact that Peter, like Jesus, was arrested for a political offense, and hence, the leaders of the Jews had to assemble a political Sanhedrin. Stephen, on the other hand, was arrested for a religious offense. Thus, he was brought before the constituted religious Sanhedrin which was daily in session. With this point of view, that Peter was arrested for a political offense, and Stephen for a religious offense, we may better understand the narrative as it is in The Acts. In the trial of Peter the Book of Acts tells us that a Sanhedrin was assembled, while in the trial of Stephen there is no mention of the fact that the high priest assembled a Sanhedrin.

According to The Acts, Stephen was stoned. There is still a question among scholars: Was Stephen stoned by verdict of the Sanhedrin, or was he merely lynched at the hands of a mob? However, there is a likelihood that he might have been stoned as a result of the court verdict since he was considered "a beguiler." He preached the doctrine that Jesus had changed the laws and customs handed down by Moses. For the first time we have a follower of the Nazarene group proclaiming that Jesus came to change the laws of Moses which, according to the Jewish conception, could not be changed, for they were eternal. Hence, Stephen was considered in the eyes of the Jews as "a beguiler" and "a deceiver."

The Book of Acts relates further that Stephen, after his lengthy speech to the members of the Sanhedrin, uttered the following words: "Behold I see the skies open and the Son of Man standing on the right hand of God."[12] When the people heard Stephen speak these words, "They cried out with loud voice, and shut their ears, and rushed together against him, and threw him out of the city and began to stone him." According to the Synoptic Gospels, when Jesus stood before the Sanhedrin and the high priest asked him: "Art thou the Christ, the Son of the Blessed?" He retorted, according to the Gospels, "and ye shall see the Son of Man sitting on the right hand of Power, and coming on the clouds of heaven." According to Mark and Matthew, the high priest considered this utterance of Jesus blasphemy.

There is a vast difference between the words of Jesus and the statement of Stephen. Jesus made a prediction while Stephen made a statement that he saw the Son of Man standing on the right hand of God; that is, he considered Jesus the founder of a new religion.

If Stephen was stoned by the verdict of the court, he was not put to death because of this particular statement only. These words would still be in the category of blasphemy, and according to the *Tannaitic* law he could not be put to death by a court. Such offense was punishable only by divine visitation. The Sanhedrin could condemn him to death only for preaching the doctrine that Jesus had the power to change the laws and customs handed down by God to Moses.

The phrase, "and they threw him out of the city and began to stone him," is in contradiction to the procedure of execution as recorded in the Talmud. Hence, some scholars take the point of view that Stephen was stoned by the people—not by the order of the Sanhedrin. It is possible that some zealots who were in the council room did not wait for the verdict of the Sanhedrin after they heard this utterance of Stephen: "Behold I see the skies open and the Son of man standing on the right hand of God," but executed him without its sanction.

The account given in The Acts of the trials of Peter and Stephen supplies additional conclusive proof that, beside the Sanhedrin which tried religious offenders, there was also a Sanhedrin which was summoned by the head of the state to try people who committed offenses against the state. This, as we have already learned, was the political Sanhedrin.

CHAPTER XII

THE TRIALS OF PAUL

IN THE trials of Peter and Stephen, the Roman authorities were not mentioned at all. This was not necessary in the case of Stephen, since he was tried before a religious Sanhedrin for a religious offense. Although Peter was tried by a political Sanhedrin for a political offense, the lack of mention of the Roman authorities in connection with his trial can readily be explained.

Peter did not cause any disturbance in Jerusalem nor in the Temple. He was arrested for disobeying the injunction of the high priest and the Sadducees against preaching the idea of resurrection, maintaining that Jesus arose from the dead and was exalted by God to be the Ruler and the Saviour of the Jews. When the high priest summoned the Sanhedrin, one of the Jewish leaders, Gamaliel, appealed to the members of the council, saying that if Peter was a rebel against the state like Theudas and Judas the Galilean, his preaching would come to nothing and he would be killed like them, but that if he "be of God" he was to be let alone. His speech had great influence over the members of the council, and they released him.

In the trials of Paul, the Roman authorities figured prominently. The names of the procurators, Felix and Festus, were mentioned often. Paul, as is well known, laid greatest stress upon the religious aspect of Jesus, on universalism against nationalism. He did not mention Jesus, the King of the Jews; neither did he call Jesus the Ruler of the Jews as Peter did.

Paul is known in history as the Apostle to the Gentiles. His early ministry, however, was in the Jewish synagogues of the Diaspora. When Paul came to Pisidian Antioch, he preached in a Jewish synagogue that Jesus was indeed the Saviour and that he was the scion of the family of David.[1] Thus, in the early days, Paul's ministry was among the Jews of the Diaspora, and he stressed at that time the idea that Jesus was a descendant of the Jewish royal family, which would have been considered a political offense against the Roman state. As a matter of fact, when Paul came to Thessalonica (*Saloniki*) and preached in the synagogue, the complaint against him and his associates was that they acted contrary to the decrees of Caesar by saying: "There is another king, Jesus."[2] Thus, we see that Paul was indeed accused of a political offense.

Paul left the Jews, and went to teach the Gospel of Jesus to the Gentiles, only when he met strong opposition among the Jews, as the author of The Acts informs us: "And when they opposed him and reviled he shook out his garments, and said to them, 'Your blood be on your head; I am clean. Henceforth I will go to the Gentiles.' "[3]

In the early period of Christianity, neither the Jews nor the Romans could clearly mark the growing separation of two distinct groups in the Church, the Jewish Christian and the Gentile Christian. The Jewish Christian group in Jerusalem was the more numerous and powerful, and to them Jesus was a Messiah, the Ruler of the Jews. They were the adherents of Jesus, who had been put to death by Pilate, for claiming to be the King of the Jews. According to Eusebius (the historian of the Church), Emperor Domitian sought to put to death Jude, the younger brother of Jesus, because he was a descendant of the Jewish royal family of King David.[4] Even at the end of the first century, the Roman authorities still looked upon the Christian Church as a political body, since it considered Jesus the Messiah, a member of the Jewish royal family. The Roman authorities were keenly suspicious of the Christians, since Jesus their Messiah was crucified by Pilate for claiming to be the King of the Jews.

In examining the passages in The Acts dealing with the arrest of Paul, we shall show that Paul, like Jesus and Peter, was arrested for a political offense and was examined only by a political Sanhedrin. In The Acts an account given by Paul while his name was still Saul, i.e., before his acceptance of Jesus, informs us that he persecuted the followers of Jesus in Jerusalem, and also received letters from the high priest to authorities in Damascus "in order that he might bring bound to Jerusalem whomsoever he found that were of the Way, both men and women."[5]

The fact that Paul obtained letters from the high priest, the head of the state, to the authorities of Damascus, to enable him to bring the followers of Jesus to Jerusalem for punishment, indicates that the adherents of Jesus were considered offenders against the state. The right to extradite any Jews who violated the law of the country was based upon an old diplomatic treaty between Rome and the Jewish state. From I Maccabbees we learn that during the time of Simon the Hasmonean, the Romans granted the Jewish state the right to extradite and to punish according to the Jewish law any "pestilent fellows" who had fled from Judea to the Roman province.[6] On the strength of this diplomatic treaty, the high priest, as head of the puppet government of the Jewish state, had demanded from the authorities of Damascus that those men be turned over to Paul to be extradited to Jerusalem for punishment.

Again, if the followers of Jesus were considered religious offenders, why did Paul obtain letters from the high priest? He should have taken them from the Sanhedrin of seventy-one, which was the highest judicial body. Furthermore, Paul said that he had scourged the men who had followed Jesus and put some of them in jail. There is no law in the Bible or in the *Tannaitic* literature punishing anyone by imprisonment for a religious offense. If these men whom Paul scourged committed a religious offense, they would have been flogged by the *Bet Din* (the court). No individual person outside of the court had the right to flog a man for a religious offense. In case, however, a person committed an offense against the state, no established rule about the nature of the punishment existed. Anyone who was delegated by the authorities of the state to inflict punishment could follow his own whim in doing so.

The first actual conflict between Paul and the Jews occurred in the city of Corinth when they accused him of persuading men to worship God contrary to the law.

The Jews of Corinth brought Paul before the Bench of Gallio, the proconsul of Achaia.[7]

The Jewish religion was privileged by the Roman Caesars to function without disturbance in the Roman Empire, but not to make converts among the Romans, and no other cults were tolerated in the Empire.[8] Apparently, when Gallio heard the complaint of the Jews against Paul, he thought that it was due only to a difference of beliefs in the Jewish religion, and not that Paul promulgated a new religion, and hence he dismissed him. Gallio said to the Jews: "If it were a matter of wrong or wicked lewdness, O ye Jews, reason would that I should bear with you: But if it be a question of words and names, and of your law, look ye to it; for I will be no judge of such matters."[9]

When Paul came to Jerusalem, he took into the Temple a number of men who purified themselves and completed the days of purification. The Jews of Asia who were in the Temple Court, seeing Paul with the men in the Temple, started a disturbance by calling to the people: "Men of Israel, help: This is the man, that teacheth all men everywhere against the people, and the law, and this place: and, further, brought Greeks also into the Temple, and hath polluted this holy place."[10] It was a capital offense, sustained by the Roman authorities, for a pagan to enter the Temple Court. Signs were placed in front of the Temple, with inscriptions in Greek and Latin, prohibiting non-Jews from entering the holy place under penalty of death.[11] This injunction and penalty applied even to Roman citizens.

As a result of the protests of the Jews of Asia crying out for help against the action of Paul, a great disturbance began in the Temple Court and in the city of Jerusalem proper. When the captain of the cohort became aware of the rioting, he came with his soldiers to the scene of the disturbance and arrested Paul. The first question which the captain put before Paul was the following: "Art not thou that Egyptian, which before these days madest an uproar, and leddest out into the wilderness four thousand men of the *Sicarii*."[12] From the query of the captain we may readily conclude that he considered Paul a political offender against the Roman state.

In previous chapters the political outlook of the *Sicarii* has been described. They were a strong political party given to terroristic methods and opposed not only to the Roman state, but also to the men who favored peace with the Romans. Against the *Sicarii*, Felix had sent out heavily armed infantry and cavalry in order to destroy them.

To the captain's question, whether Paul was the Egyptian or connected with the *Sicarii*, Paul replied that he was a Jew born in Tarsus and that he was "a citizen of no mean city." With this reply, Paul dismissed both accusations, because, since he was born in Tarsus, he could not have been connected with "the Egyptian," and, since he was a citizen of Tarsus, a Roman province, he could not have been associated with the *Sicarii* who were Judeans fighting for their national home against Rome.

The captain was anxious to find out the true cir-

cumstances of the accusation brought by the Jews against
Paul. He commanded that the high priests and their
Sanhedrin assemble. When Paul was brought before the
Sanhedrin to be examined, and learned that one group
of them consisted of Sadducees and the other of Pharisees, he cried out to the Sanhedrin: "Brethren, I am
a Pharisee, a son of a Pharisee: of the hope and resurrection of the dead I am judged."[13] The fact that some
members of the Sanhedrin consisted of Sadducees and
some were Pharisees proves undoubtedly that the Sanhedrin was not a religious body, but a political Sanhedrin, and that Paul was brought before it for a
political offense. It would be unthinkable to assume
that a religious court would consist of Sadducees and
Pharisees, since their beliefs were so diametrically opposed to each other, for what would appear to the
Pharisees a religious offense would not be so considered
by the Sadducees. It would be very much as if, in our
own days, a person accused of a transgression against
the Church would be tried by a synod composed of
Catholics and Protestants. What would be considered
a religious transgression by the Catholics would not
be considered such by the Protestants.

But if we assume that Paul was brought before a
political Sanhedrin—as I have already shown to have
been the case with Jesus—we can understand why its
members consisted of Sadducees and Pharisees. It was
quite proper for the head of a nation to convene citizens of different religious beliefs for the purpose of
trying a man for a state offense. Furthermore, Paul
could not have been brought before the religious San-

hedrin as he did not commit a religious transgression.
He was accused of bringing a pagan into the Temple
Court. Paul himself, as a Jew, had the full right to be
in the Temple. According to *Tannaitic* Halakah (law),
an accomplice was not punishable by a court.[14]

Paul's shrewd move in stating to the members of the
Sanhedrin that he had been brought before them because he believed in resurrection was successful. Indeed, the *Soferim*, the learned men of the Pharisees,
openly declared that they saw nothing wrong in Paul's
words.[15] A great disturbance started between the Pharisees and the Sadducees. It is known that the question
of resurrection was sharply debated between these two
sects. Resurrection was not only a theological difference
between them; their entire mode of life was motivated
by their belief or disbelief in it. Even their ritual and
criminal codes were influenced by their attitude toward
resurrection.

When the captain, Lysias, received word of the disturbance, he placed Paul in a military fortress as he
was afraid that Paul might "be torn in pieces." Some
Jews, apparently fanatics, "put themselves under curse
(*herem*)," that they would not eat or drink until they
had killed Paul. They informed the high priests and
the elders of their *herem* and advised them that they
should make a representation to the captain to send
Paul to the elders for another examination, so that they
might kill him on the way.[16] This plot became known
to Paul who notified the captain. The latter, perplexed by the case and not knowing how to handle it,
since Paul was a Roman citizen, decided to send Paul

to the procurator, Felix. The captain wrote a letter to the procurator stating the facts of the case. The letter, as it is given in The Acts, states,

Claudius Lysias unto the most excellent governor Felix sendeth greeting. This man was taken of the Jews, and should have been killed of them: then came I with an army, and rescued him, having understood that he was a Roman. And when I would have known the cause wherefore they accused him, I brought him forth into their Sanhedrin: Whom I perceived to be accused of questions of their law, but to have nothing laid to his charge worthy of death or of bonds. And when it was told me how that the Jews laid wait for the man, I sent straightway to thee, and gave commandment to his accusers also to say before thee what they had against him. Farewell.[17]

When Lysias sent Paul to Felix, he ordered the Jewish leaders to proceed to Caesarea to make their complaints against Paul before the procurator. Ananias, the high priest, went to Caesarea with some elders and a pleader by the name of Tertullus, who placed the charges against Paul before the procurator. He accused him of being a nuisance (pestilent)[18] and causing insurrections among the Jews throughout the world; of being the leader of the party of the Nazarenes and of attempting to defile the Temple, for all of which he was seized.[19] The first two accusations were of a political character. The third accusation was purely religious— that he was the leader of the party of the Nazarenes. The last accusation concerning the pagans in the prohibited area, however, was a political offense, since the Roman authorities prohibited any pagan, even a Roman citizen, from entering the Temple Court.

Paul flatly denied all the accusations. He argued that
the only offense that the Sanhedrin actually found
against him during his examination before them was
his belief in resurrection.[20] Felix, after he had heard
the arguments, reserved judgment until the time when
Captain Lysias would come to him to report. In the
meantime he commanded that Paul was to be held in
prison.

When Felix's successor, Festus, came to Jerusalem,
the high priest and some of the Jewish leaders laid
information before him against Paul, and urged him
to send Paul from Caesarea to Jerusalem. According
to The Acts, the reason that some of the leaders asked
Festus to bring Paul to Jerusalem was for the purpose
of killing him on the way.[21] According to the Har-
clean[22] margin, it was the same men who had previously put a curse on themselves to kill Paul who now
asked Festus to bring Paul to Jerusalem. Festus, however, declined their request, and told them that Paul
was being held in Caesarea and that the Jewish dignitaries should go there. "Let them accuse him," he said.[23]

Festus, upon returning to Caesarea, ordered an inquiry into Paul's case. Paul was brought in before the
tribunal. The Jewish dignitaries who came from Jerusalem laid their charges against him. Apparently, the
same accusations that were brought against Paul at the
time of the inquiry before Felix were brought forward
again. According to The Acts, the Jews could not prove
their charges against Paul. He again flatly denied these
charges, which were of a political nature, by saying,
"Neither against the law of the Jaws, neither against

the temple, nor yet against Caesar, have I offended any-
thing at all."[24]

It is apparent that Paul not only did not deny the
religious accusation but affirmed it. This hypothesis
can be substantiated by the account given in The Acts.
When Festus told King Agrippa about the trial of Paul,
he said: "(They) had certain questions against him of
their own religion (demon worship), and of one Jesus,
which was dead whom Paul affirmed to be alive."[25] This
shows that Paul affirmed the religious accusation that
was brought against him, that he was the leader of the
party of the Nazarenes. Festus, perplexed entirely by
the accusation and not able to apprehend that Jesus
arose from the dead, decided on a change of venue, to
transfer the trial to Jerusalem. Since the incident for
which Paul was arrested, namely for attempting to defile the Temple, had taken place in Jerusalem, and
the captain who had arrested him was also in Jerusalem,
it was therefore proper to hold the inquiry in that
city.

When Festus asked Paul, "Wilt thou go up to Jerusalem, and there be judged of these things (charges)
before me?"[26] Paul declined and said, "I stand at
Caesar's judgment seat (tribunal) where I ought to be
judged: to the Jews have I done no wrong."[27] From the
reply of Paul to Festus we may assume that Festus
wanted to release Paul to the Jews to be tried also for
a religious offense, in addition to the trial before the
procurator for the political offense.

This theory that Festus was willing to release Paul
to the Jews to be tried for the religious offense can

be further substantiated. When Festus related to Agrippa his perplexity about Paul's utterance that Jesus arose from the dead, he told Agrippa that he asked Paul to "go to Jerusalem and there be tried on these matters." The phrase, "to try him there on these matters," referred to the accusation about the "resurrection." This charge was of a religious character, and the Roman government never interfered with the religious customs of the Jews. The Jews had full religious freedom, and so Paul would have had to be tried before the religious Sanhedrin and not before Festus. Hence, we may assume that Festus was ready to release Paul to the Jews to be tried for a religious offense. By appealing to Caesar, Paul now compelled Festus to transfer him to Rome to be tried there before Caesar.

The entire issue was not very clear to Festus. It was very complicated since there were political as well as religious charges against Paul. Festus did not know how to prepare the report for Caesar. When King Agrippa and his sister, Bernice, paid a visit to Caesarea, Festus told them about Paul. Agrippa became interested and asked Festus if he could meet Paul. Paul related to the king the history of his life before he had joined Jesus and told him of the charges which were brought against him and his beliefs in the matter of resurrection. Agrippa said to Festus: "This man might have been set at liberty, if he had not appealed unto Caesar."[28] The author of The Acts does not tell us how Paul's life ended.

Early Christian tradition, however, informs us that Paul was beheaded by Nero Caesar. This tradition that

Paul was beheaded in Rome was universally held in the early Church. The Church historian, Eusebius, states that Paul suffered martyrdom in Rome under Nero. He gives, as his authority, the church father, Origen[29] (at the beginning of the third century). And the church father, Tertullian (at the end of the second century), records that Paul was beheaded in Rome.[30] Eusebius states that Peter was crucified in Rome under Nero.[31] He also quotes Origen as authority for the crucifixion of Peter in Rome. The Book of Acts, however, does not record the martyrdom of Peter and Paul.

The author of The Acts, in relating the trials of Paul, pictured the Jews as the persecutors of Paul, seeking to destroy him, while Felix and Festus tried to save him. However, we learn about the character of these two men, Felix and Festus, not only from Josephus but from the Roman historian Tacitus.

Tacitus said that Felix "practiced every kind of cruelty and lust,[32] . . . fostering crime by misconceived remedies."[33] We know from Josephus that Felix mercilessly crucified anyone who associated himself with those who were against the Roman state. The account dealing with Paul reveals bitter animosity toward the Jews. This hostility in The Acts can be readily explained if we take into consideration the time when, and the people for whom the book was written. Most of the New Testament scholars agree that the Book of Acts was compiled after the destruction of the Temple, between the years 100 and 130 C.E.[34]

The author of The Acts made use of Josephus' work *The Wars of the Jews*. It has been mentioned before that the author of The Acts used the word *Sicarii*. The word *Sicarii* is Latin and Josephus was the first writer in the Greek literature to use it. The word *Sicarii* was never used before Josephus in Greek literature. Hence, it is quite evident that the author of The Acts must have made use of *The Wars of the Jews*, which was written after the destruction of the Temple. At that time the Jews had been totally destroyed politically, and thousands upon thousands were taken captive and sold into slavery. The Acts, particularly the second part which deals with Paul, was written not for the Jewish Christians but for the Gentile Christians. The author emphasized the fact that Paul was the Apostle to the Gentiles who preached the Gospel of Jesus as the Saviour of mankind.

The compiler of The Acts, who wrote with the Romans in mind and with the idea of recruiting converts among them, could not accuse the Roman authorities of persecuting Paul. We have pointed out the same motive in the Gospel according to John, where the animosity against the Jews was very outspoken. Since that gospel was written for the Gentile Christians, the evangelist wanted to convey the idea to the Gentiles that the Jews, who rejected the gospel, had killed the Master. The author of The Acts tried to dissociate Paul's Christianity from purely Jewish religion so that the Romans should not look upon a convert to Christianity as one who belonged to the rebels, the Jews.[35]

This was why the author of The Acts was silent about the martyrdom of Peter and Paul at the hands of Nero Caesar, since the early Christians sought to ingratiate themselves with the Romans. There can be no doubt that when the book was compiled, the martyrdom of Peter and Paul was well known to the members of the Church, since the martyrdom of these two pillars of the Church occurred at least three decades before the compilation of The Acts.

The accusation which at most may be brought against the Jewish leaders who were responsible to the Roman authorities was that they delivered Paul to the Romans. An interesting passage in chapter 21 of The Acts relates that, when Paul came to Caesarea and stayed with Philip, he was warned not to proceed to Jerusalem, by a prophet from Judea who foretold that the Jews "shall deliver him (Paul) into the hands of the Gentiles."[36] From this prediction as recorded in The Acts we learn that the only accusation against the Jews was that they *delivered* Paul to the Romans. The author of The Acts does not say that the prophet from Judea predicted that the Jews would try to *kill* Paul. Even the delivery of Paul to the Romans was forced by political circumstances, since the Jewish leaders were under the Roman yoke and were responsible to the Roman rulers for the political tranquillity of the country.

CHAPTER XIII

HISTORY—MAGISTRA VITAE

"HISTORY is the teacher of life," said Cicero. By this he meant that a knowledge of the past enables men to understand the present, and even to predict events of the future. But, is it not equally true that, as we comprehend better the nature of mankind, the forces that operate within human society, the motives of men leading them to glory or despair, the present illumines the dark and hidden places of the past? The common denominator of all history is human nature, relatively the same throughout the ages. Hence, the historian is justified in asserting that contemporary history takes us by the hand and leads us through the mazes, the perplexities, the mysteries of bygone ages, and enables us to reconstruct the past with ever greater verisimilitude of the truth.

Surely, no event needs greater illumination than the trial, crucifixion and death of Jesus of Nazareth. Its centrality in Christian civilization requires it; its meaning for world history seeks it; its effect upon the Jewish people demands it. Scholarship can untangle the texts and research can reconstruct the background, but only an appreciation of the living forces and powers that rise from struggling and questing humanity can breathe the vital spirit of life into text and background and event. The sorrows and tragedies of our world and our times, strange as it may seem, can cast a white and shining light upon the heights of Calvary, dark with the cross and the crucified Jesus. Never in all history have times been more analogous than our own to those that prevailed in the time of the crucifixion of the Nazarene.

As today many small states have been overrun by the Nazis, and lie in anguish beneath their bloody heel, so ancient Judea was conquered by imperial Rome and writhed beneath her iron-shod legions. As today, patriots of these countries are tortured and killed by their conquerors, so the Apocalyptists and the *Sicarii* fought and suffered for the liberation of their state from Roman oppressors. As modern Quislings, puppet governments and puppet rulers, betray their peoples and become instruments to work the will of the conqueror, so in a world now passed away Jewish Quislings proved traitors to their own people that they might, for personal aggrandizement and power, do the bidding of Roman masters.

Scholars, in their attempt to explain the crucifixion of Jesus, have sought devious and ingenious ways to pierce to the heart of the mystery. Some have tried to place the blame on the Sadducees, hoping thus to exonerate the Pharisees, and, by implication, the modern Jews who are the historical heirs of the Pharisees. Others have sought to exculpate the individual Jew of modern times by placing the burden of guilt of the death of Jesus upon the Jews as a people. Not only do these explanations reveal an ignorance of Jewish history, but, as apologist, they are based upon distortions of history, and hence must be false and harmful.

Only upon truth can the house of mankind be securely builded.

We have learned that the Sadducees had no judicial or political power, and, therefore, they could not have committed the crime of Jesus' death. They were one group within the Jewish people that differed from the Pharisees theologically and politically. Yet, they were an integral part of the Jewish people. The Pharisees, on the other hand, despite their hostility to the Sadducees, never put any of them to death for disbelief in the Oral Law or in resurrection. At most, they maintained that those who did not believe in these matters would have no portion in the future world.

But, to set the blame on a party of the Jewish people cannot exonerate the whole Jewish people from responsibility for the crucifixion, any more than an act by a Republican President and Congress or by a Democratic President and Congress frees the entire American people from total responsibility for such act.

To say, as does Renan, the French orientalist and the author of *The Life of Jesus*, that, while the individual Jew of modern days cannot be blamed for the crucifixion of Jesus eighteen centuries ago, the Jews as a nation must carry the blame, is but to play with words and let realities slip through them. Without individuals, there can be no such entity as a people; the nation as such is a shadowy unreality without the flesh and sinew of distinctive individuals.

Our task has been to make clear that neither Pharisees nor Sadducees, nor the Jewish people as a whole, could be held responsible, even morally, for the crucifixion of Jesus. Jesus was crucified by the Romans for a political offense as the King of the Jews. No fair-minded student of contemporaneous affairs would hold the Norwegian people responsible for the murder of patriots by Quisling who rules under the protection of his German overlord. No impartially minded judge today would blame the Czech nation for the killing of their own patriots by the Germans with the help of the puppet government of Hacha, so-called president of the Czech Protectorate. So, the facts and realities of history exculpate the Jewish people from the burden of guilt for the crucifixion of Jesus, for they were bowed beneath the yoke of Rome, ruled by evil procurators who held power of life and death over them, and gave protection to Jewish Quislings—the high priests—who served their and Rome's purposes.

Indeed, even upon Pilate alone the entire blame for the crucifixion of Jesus cannot be set. Men are oft-times the victims of their own systems. Inherent in the very nature of imperialism are evil forces that distort men's natures, that give rise to cruelties and terrorisms, that compel men to degrade and use other men to nefarious ends. The system of Roman imperialism and the destruction of small nations inevitably brought about their Pilates, their Quislings, and their crucified victims. As long as imperialism exists, there are bound to be traitors and betrayers who will help the conqueror to destroy those men who are working and sacrificing for the liberty of their countries. The death of Jesus at the hands of Pontius Pilate was but another example of how victim and oppressor were equally the resultants and creatures of a universal evil, imperialism.

There is a popular saying that, "History repeats

itself." As a matter of fact, history does not really repeat itself; only the writers of history repeat themselves. History is an ever-flowing river of events, in which the forces of good and evil struggle for supremacy. It zigzags through time, winding in and out, submerged during moments of darkness, only to emerge into daylight in happier places. Names of men and places change, scenes of conflict and individuals vary, but the eternal struggle under new names continues unabated.

The dark forces that fought in the first century against ideals of the universality of God, the equality of man, and freedom for all humanity, still battle against them in our midst today. The paganism of Rome in new and different garb is still alive. The cruelties of Caligula and Nero against those who believed in and preached the ideas of a supreme God and that all mankind is equal before God, are still indulged in by the pagan spirit. The ideas and ideals which were given voice on the hills of Judea and on the mount of Galilee are not yet fulfilled, due to the same forces of greed, cruelty, hate and reaction which existed in the time of Jesus. The dark forces of the first century are still with us in the twentieth century.

Cicero well said, "History is the teacher of life." By that teacher, provided we learn the lessons of the past, we might be helped to build a better life today. If we were truly blessed with wisdom and farsighted leadership, we might create, through the fulfillment of the teachings of the Bible, a new and better world tomorrow.

NOTES

INTRODUCTION

1. *Fertur Titus adhibito consilio prius deliberasse an templum tanti operis everteret. Etenim nonnullis videbatur aedem sacratam ultra omnia mortalia inlustrem non oportere deleri, quae servata modestiae Romanae testimonium, diruta perennem crudelitatis notam praeberet. At contra alii et Titus ipse evertendum in primis templum censebant quo plenius Iudaeorum et Christianorum religio tolleretur: quippe has religiones, licet contrarias sibi, isdem tamen ab auctoribus profectas; Christianos ex Iudaeis extitisse: radice sublata stirpem facile perituram. (Fragmenta Historiarum, Sulpicius Severus, Chron. II.30:6)*

CHAPTER 2

1. Ezra 1:1-3.
2. *Ibid.*, 7:1-5.
3. I Kings 2:35.
4. The word "theocracy" as a state ruled by priests was first coined by Josephus in his book *Against Apion*.
5. Num. 25:11-13.
6. Deut. 33:8-10.
7. Gen. 49:8-11.
8. See *Talmud Temurah* 16a.
9. See S. Zeitlin, *The History of the Second Jewish Commonwealth, Prolegomena*.
10. Polybius 5:86; Bevan, *The House of Seleucus* chap. 10; *idem. History of Egypt* chap. 7.
11. S. Zeitlin, *op. cit.*
12. Josephus *Ant.* 12.
13. II Macc. 4:19.
14. I Macc. 1:20-24. See Clinton, *Fasti Hellenici* 3:318-320.
15. I Macc. 1:20-64; II Macc. 5.
16. *Ibid.*, 6.
17. *Ibid.*, 7.
18. Ben Sirah, 47, 11.

19. I Macc. 2:57.
20. Psalms 132. See also Psalm 89:21-38. In II Chron. 18:14 David is called the man of God.
21. II Macc. 7:9.
22. *Ibid.*, 36-37.
23. *Talmud Yoma* 85; *Makiltha. Tractate Shabboth* 1.
24. I Macc. 1:32.
25. *Ibid.*, 14:27-42.
26. This is the reason why Josephus did not mention the Pharisees up to the time of the Hasmoneans.
27. *Talmud Menahoth* 65a.
28. *Ibid.* See Zeitlin, *op. cit.*
29. *Idem.*
30. *Mishnah Menahoth* 10:3; See S. Zeitlin *op. cit.*
31. *Ibid.*
32. Exod. 16:29.
33. *Tosefta Erubin* 7:3; 4:9,11.
34. Acts. 1:12.
35. *Mekiltha, Tractate Shabbath* 1.
36. Isa. 58:13.
37. M. S. Enslin, *Christian Beginnings* p. 116.
38. Lev. 15:16; *ibid.*, 22:7; Deut. 23:11-12; Compare I Sam. 20:25-26.
39. *Sifra Shemini* 8; *Emor.* 4:1.
40. See S. Zeitlin, *The Pharisees and the Gospels.*
41. Lev. 11:38.
42. *Tosefta Makshirin* 3:3; *Sifra Shemini* 11; Compare *Mishnah Yadaim* 4.

CHAPTER 3

1. I Macc. 16; Josephus, *Ant.* 13:7.
2. *Ibid.*, 13:9-10; *Jewish War* 1:2,6-7
3. See S. Zeitlin, *An Historical Study of the Canonization of the Hebrew Scriptures* pp. 1-2.
4. *Ant.* 13:10,6.
5. *Ibid.*, "The Pharisees have delivered to the people a great many observances by succession from their fathers, which are not written in the laws of Moses; and for that reason it is that the Sadducees reject them, and say, that we are to esteem those observances to be obligatory which are in the

written word, but are not to observe what are derived from the tradition of our forefathers. And concerning these things it is that great disputes and differences have arisen among them, while the Sadducees are able to persuade none but the rich, and have not the populace obsequious to them, but the Pharisees have the multitude on their side."

6. See S. Zeitlin, *The History of the Second Jewish Commonwealth, Prolegomena.*
7. *Ant.* 13:11.
8. *Jewish War* 1:4,6.
9. *Talmud Sota* 22b.
10. *Ant.* 13:16.
11. *Ibid.,* 14:1,3.
12. *Ibid.,* 14:3,2.
13. *Ibid.,* 14:4,3. See also S. Zeitlin, *Megillat Taanit* chap. 3.
14. Julius 11.
15. *Ibid.,* 35.
16. Tacitus, *Annals* 2:59; *idem. Histories* 1:11.
17. *Ant.* 14.8.
18. *Ibid.,* 14:9.
19. *Ibid.*
20. *Ibid.,* 14:16; See S. Zeitlin *op. cit.*
21. *Ant.* 15:1.
22. *Ibid.,* 15:2.
23. *Ibid.,* 15:3.
24. *Ibid.,* 15:10,4.
25. *Ibid.*
26. *Ibid.,* 15, 6.
27. *Ibid.,* 16, 11.
28. *Ibid.,* 15, 7:7.
29. *Talmud Baba-Batrab* 3b.
30. *Ant.* 15:7,4. "For as the king was one day about noon laid down on his bed to rest him, he called Mariamne, out of the great affection he had always for her. She came in accordingly, but would not lie down by him; and when he was very desirous of her company, she showed her contempt of him."
31. *Jewish War* 1:33,6
32. *Ibid.*
33. *Ibid.,* 2:6,2.

34. *Ibid.*
35. *Ibid.*, 8.
36. *Ant.* 18:1; *Jewish War* 2:8,1.
37. Philo, *Embassy to Gaius* 38.
38. *Jewish War* 2:9,2-3.
39. Luke 13:1.
40. *Jewish War* 2:9,4.
41. *Ibid.*, 2:10,1-5.
42. *Histories* 5:10.
43. *Vespasian* 4. "There had spread over all the Orient an old and established belief, that it was fated at that time for men coming from Judea to rule the world."
44. Tacitus, *Histories* 5:13; *Jewish War* 6:5,4.
45. *Claudius* 25. "Since the Jews constantly made disturbances at the instigation of *Chrestus*, he expelled them from Rome."
46. *Ant.* 19:8,1-2.
47. *Ibid.*, 20:1.
48. *Ibid.*, 20:5.
49. *Ibid.*
50. *Histories* 5:9.
51. *Ant.* 20:8,6.
52. *Ibid.*, 8,5.
53. *Ibid.*
54. *Jewish War* 4:6,1.

CHAPTER 4

1. Herodotus 1,105.
2. See *Talmud Sota* 48.
3. *Ibid.* See S. Zeitlin, the *Am-Harez, Jewish Quarterly Review,* 1932.
4. *Tosefta Menahoth* 13:21.
5. The Jewish Commonwealth was called *Heber-Hayehudim* which means Association of Jews.
6. *Mishnah and Tosefta Demai, Talmud Hagigah* 22b.
7. See S. Zeitlin *op. cit.*
8. *Jewish War* 3:3,2.
9. *Ibid.*
10. John 7:52; compare *Erubin* 53a; *Palestinian Talmud Shabbath* 16:8.
11. *Ibid.*, 7,41.

CHAPTER 5

1. See Chapter II, present volume.
2. See S. Zeitlin, *The History of the Second Jewish Commonwealth.*
3. *Mishnah Sanhedrin* 1:1; *Tosefta Hagigah* 2:9.
4. S. Zeitlin, *Jewish Quarterly Review* 1939.
5. *Idem.*
6. *Mishnah Sanhedrin* 1:1.
7. *Tosefta Hagigah* 2:9.
8. *Mishnah Sanhedrin* 4:1.
9. *Ant.* 14,9:3-4; *Jewish War* 1:10,6.
10. *Talmud Kiddushin* 43a.
11. *Ibid.*
12. *Ant.* 16:6,2.
13. *Mishnah Sanhedrin* 7:1.
14. *Tosefta Sanhedrin* 7:1; *Palestinian Talmud ibid.*
15. *Ant.* 18:1,4.
16. *Tosefta Nidah* 5:3; *Talmud ibid.*, 33a; *Yoma* 19b.
17. The statement in the Talmud that the Jews lost their right to pronounce sentence of death forty years before the destruction of the Temple cannot be taken as historical fact, since we have many statements in the *Tannaitic* literature to the contrary. See my study in the *Jewish Quarterly Review*, 1941. Compare Jean Juster, *Les Juifs dans l'Émpire Romain* Vol. II, pp. 132-145.
18. *Mishnah Sanhedrin* 7:2.
19. *Jewish War* 6,2,4; *ibid.*, 5:5,2.
20. *Ibid.* See Dissmann, *Light from the Ancient East*, 1927.
21. *Delegation to Gaius*, 38.
22. *Jewish War* 2:11,6.
23. See Th. Mommson, *the History of Rome* part 2, chap. 11; also Juster *op. cit.*
24. *Jewish War* 1:10,6; *hoc lib.* Chapter III.
25. *Talmud Sanhedrin* 48b.
26. *Ant.* 15:6,2.
27. *Ibid.*, 15:7,4. According to the account given in the *Jewish War* 1:22,3, Herod killed Mariamne without any trial.
28. *Jewish War* 1:27,2.
29. *Ibid.*, 1,29,2.

30. *Ant.* 20:9,6.
31. *Ibid.,* 20.9,1; See also my study *Jewish Quarterly Review,* 1941.
32. *Jewish War* 4:5,4.

CHAPTER 6

1. Chapter II, present volume.
2. *Ant.* 13:10,6.
3. Acts 23:8.
4. *Jewish War* 2:8,14.
5. *Ant.* 13:10,6.
6. *Jewish War* 2:8,14.
7. *Ant.* 13:10,6.
8. *Ibid.*
9. *Talmud Sota* 48. See Chapter II, present volume.
10. *On the Virtuous Being also Free* 12; *Fragments.*
11. *Jewish War* 2:8,2; *Ant.* 13:8,2. A description of the Essenes is also given by Pliny the Elder. See E. Schürer, *A History of the Jewish People.*
12. See, *The Beginnings of Christianity* Part 1, edited by F. J. Foakes Jackson and Kirsopp Lake; W. F. Albright, *From the Stone Age to Christianity* pp. 288-290.
13. See Schürer *op. cit.*
14. *Jewish War* 2:8,2.
15. *Ibid.*
16. *Ant.* 18:1,6.
17. *Ibid.*
18. *Jewish War* 7:8,1; 2:13,3,17,6; 4:7,2; 7:8,4-5.
19. *Ant.* 18:1,6.
20. *Jewish War* 7:8,6-7.
21. *Ibid.*
22. See my essay, *Josephus, Patriot or Traitor.*
23. *Ant.* 20:9,3.
24. *Jewish War* 2:13,4-6.
25. *Ant.* 20:5,1.
26. *Jewish War* 2:13,5.
27. Acts 5:36; 21:38.
28. *Jewish War* 2:13,4.
29. *The Testament of the Twelve Patriarchs* (The Testament of Joseph) 18:2.

30. Matt. 24:24.
31. *Ant.* 17:2,4.
32. Josephus as we know from his works had a great admiration for the Pharisees.
33. The Psalms of Solomon 17:23; 36.
34. *Ibid.* Compare also IV Ezra 7:27; "For my son the Messiah (the Messiah of God)."
35. *Ibid.*, Book of Enoch, 48:10.
36. *Ibid.*, 49:2; 51:1.
37. *Ibid.*, 62:14; 69:26,29.
38. *Ibid.*, 69:4; "sons of God"; *ibid.*, 105:2; IV Ezra 7:27.
39. Book of Enoch 51:2.

CHAPTER 7

1. Mark 14:12; Matt. 26:2; Luke 22:7.
2. John 13:1,18,28; 19:31.
3. See C. S. Davidson, *An Introduction to the Study of the New Testament* Vol. II; see also Strack und Billerbeck, *Kommentar Zum Neuen Testament;* see also C. Torrey, the *Date of the Crucifixion According to the Fourth Gospel, Journal of Biblical Literature,* 1931 pp. 227-241; compare also my study, "The Date of the Crucifixion According to the Fourth Gospel," 1932, pp. 263-271.
4. See A. Olmstead, "The Chronology of Jesus' Life," *American Theological Review,* 1942, p. 7.
5. Eusebius, *The Church History* 3:39.
6. Justin Martyr, *Dialogue with Trypho* 72; "This Passover is our Saviour and our refuge." "And as the blood of Passover saved those who were in Egypt, so also the blood of Christ will deliver from death those who have believed" 111.
7. Epistle to the Hebrews 13:20. "Through the blood of the everlasting covenant."
8. John 1:29.
9. *Ibid.*, 19:33.
10. Exod. 12,46.
11. See W. Allen, *the Gospel According to St. Matthew;* M. S. Enslin, *Christian Beginnings* p. 400.
12. A. Harnack, *The Date of the Acts and of the Synoptic Gospels* 1911; Easton, *The Gospel before the Gospels* 1928.

13. E. Gould, *The Gospel According to St. Mark;* Enslin, *op. cit.*
14. Eusebius, *op. cit.* 2:15.
15. S. Zeitlin, *The Pharisees and the Gospels*, pp. 48-49.
16. Mark 14:62.
17. *Ibid.*, 9:5.
18. John 8:17; 10:34; 15:25.
19. *Ibid.*, 2:13; 11:55; *pass.*
20. *Ibid.*, 7:2.
21. See Enslin, *op. cit.*
22. See Plummer's *Introduction to the Gospel of St. Luke.*
23. Enslin, *op. cit.*
24. See S. Zeitlin *The Pharisees and the Gospels.*

CHAPTER 8

1. Matt. 5:38-42.
2. *Ibid.*, 5:17-18.
3. A *private delict* gives rise to an obligation; the law intends that delinquents shall be punished by becoming liable to a personal action at the suit of the injured party, the object of such action being either to recover damages or a penalty, or to recover both damages and penalty. Compare Shon's *Institutes of Roman Law.*
4. Num. 35; Deut. 19:12.
5. II Sam. 3:27; *ibid.*, 14:6-8.
6. *Ant.* 4:8,35.
7. *Talmud Baba Kamma* 83b.
8. Matt. 5:31-32; *ibid.*, 19:3-9; Mark 10:2-12; Luke 16:18.
9. Matt. 19:7-9.
10. *Mishnah Gittin* 9:10.
11. Matt. 5:27-30.
12. Deut. 23:24; compare Ben Sirah 23:9: "Accustom not thy mouth to an oath and be not accustomed to the naming of the Holy One."
13. Compare Prov. 25:21: "If thine enemy be hungry, give him bread to eat; and if he be thirsty, give him water to drink."
14. *Talmud Shabbath* 31a.
15. Tobit 4:15. Compare The Twelve Patriarchs, The Testimony of Joseph: "If any man seek to do evil unto you do him a good turn and pray for him."

CHAPTER 9

1. Matt. 12:1-8; Mark 2:23-28; Luke 6:1-5.
2. See Chapter II, present volume.
3. *Ibid.*
4. Matt. 12:22-24; Mark 3:22.
5. Matt. 9:14-15; Mark 2:18-20; Luke 5:33-35.
6. II Sam. 12:21-23.
7. *Talmud Gittin* 56a.
8. Zech. 7:3; 8:19.
9. See Chapter III, present volume.
10. Mark 7:1-13; Matt. 15:1-6.
11. Chapter II, present volume.
12. See S. Zeitlin *The Pharisees and the Gospels*, p. 29. Matthew's text reads "It is a gift" (King James Version); in Mark the reading is "*Corban* that is to say a gift." However, in some versions of the Gospel according to Mark the phrase "that is a gift" is not found, and in some versions of the Gospel according to Matthew we have the readings "Corban, that is a gift." From this we can readily see that the word "corban" was in Matthew as well. In the Syrian version of the Gospels we have the word "corban" only, and the words, "that is a gift," are omitted.

 On the basis of the readings which we have now in the Gospels most of the commentators took the word *Corban* to mean a gift, and they constructed this passage accordingly. "That by which you might have received advantage from me is hereby dedicated as an offering." The word *Corban*, however, mentioned in the Gospels, does not have the meaning of a gift but a vow. In this sense a vow is found quite often in the *Tannaitic* literature (*Mishna Nedarim* 1, *Tosefta Ibid.*), and hence this passage in Matthew should be translated accordingly, "But you say whosoever shall say to his father or to his mother a *Corban* (vow), by whatsoever thou mightest be profited by me; and honour not his father or his mother."
13. *Mishnah Nedarim* II; *Tosefta Hagigah* 1:9.
14. Matt. 9:11; Mark 2:16; Luke 5:30.
15. *Shibhe ha-BeShT*.
16. Assumption of Moses 7:2-10.
17. The name Rabbi was not known to the Jews at the time of

Jesus, and was not used by them even as a complimentary term. See Zeitlin *op. cit.*, p. 36.

18. Matt. 22:35-36; Mark 12:14,32; Luke 20:21,28,39.
19. Matt. 26:49.
20. Luke 22:47.
21. John 9:16; 11:47.
22. *Ibid.*, 12:42.
23. *Ibid.*, 7:45-50.
24. See Chapter VII, present volume.

CHAPTER 10

1. Mark 14-15.
2. Luke 22:66.
3. *Ibid.*, 23:2.
4. *Ibid.*, 23:38-40.
5. Matt. 27:19.
6. *Ibid.*, 27:24-26.
7. John 18-19.
8. *Ibid.*, 11:47-50.
9. *Talmud Keritut* 7.
10. *Mishnah Sanhedrin* 7.
11. See Psalms 110:1: "A Psalm of David, God said unto my Lord. Sit thou at my right hand."
12. *Against Verres* 5:66.
13. *Ant.* 20:5,2.
14. *Jewish War* 5:11,1.
15. *Ibid.*, 6:5,3.
16. Mark 11:9-10; compare Luke 19:38, "Blessed be the King."
17. John 12:13.
18. *Ibid.*, 6:15.
19. Mark 12:13-17.
20. This corresponds to the account given by the Synoptists, but according to John, Jesus was arrested on Thursday night, the thirteenth of Nisan.
21. See M. Goguel, *The Life of Jesus* pp. 496-497.
22. I. Cor. 15:5.
23. This custom is recorded only in the Gospels. There is no mention of it in the Talmud.
24. Suetonius, *Caligula* 32.
25. Luke 23:27.

26. Enoch 105:2.
27. Psalms 2:7; 110:1.
28. According to John, Jesus was tried on the day before Passover.
28a. The American Revised Version has "robbers."
29. Luke 12:39.
30. According to the Roman law, in the time of Jesus, the executioners took the minor spoils of those whom they crucified.
31. Mark 15:32; Matt. 27:42.
32. See S. Zeitlin, *The Jews, Race, Nation, or Religion.*
33. Tacitus, *Annals* 4.
34. *Legation to Gaius* 24; *Against Flaccus* 1.
35. Matt. 16:21.
36. Mark 8:31; Luke 9:22.
37. Mark 14:1.
38. Luke 24:20, see *Jewish Quarterly Review* 1941.
39. Acts 3:13.
40. Acts 5:30.
41. I Corinthians 2:6-8.
42. I Thessalonians 2:14-16.
43. *Annals* 15,44.

CHAPTER 11

1. Matt. 16:17-18.
2. *Ibid.,* 10:5-6. "These twelve Jesus sent forth, and commanded them saying, 'Go not into the way of the Gentiles, and into any city of the Samaritans enter ye not: But go rather to the lost sheep of the house of Israel.'"
3. Acts 4-5. On the text of this chapter, see my study in the *Jewish Quarterly Review* 1941.
4. *Ibid.,* 3:13. The words "and killed the Prince of life" Acts 3:15, cannot be taken literally, as is quite evident from other passages in Acts 3:13; Luke 24:20. Peter evidently accused the leaders of causing Jesus' death. According to the author of The Acts Peter had in mind the moral responsibility of the Jews for the death of Jesus. See above pp. 177-8.
5. Eusebius, *The Church History* 3:4; See H. Cadbury, *The Beginnings of Christianity* Vol. II ed. by Jackson and Lake; M. S. Enslin, *Christian Beginnings.*
6. Luke 24:20.
7. See my study *op. cit.*

8. Acts 5:34-39.
9. *Ant.* 20:5,1.
10. *Jewish War* 2:8,1. There is an anachronism in the account as recorded in The Acts. Fadus became procurator after 44 C.E. and hence the activities of Theudas belong to the period after Agrippa, while Judas the Galilean incited the Jews to revolt against the Romans in the year 4 C.E. at the time of Herod's death.
11. Acts 6:8-14; 7:57-59.
12. See my study *op. cit.* note 157.

CHAPTER 12

1. Acts 13:23.
2. *Ibid.,* 17:7.
3. *Ibid.,* 18:6; see my study *op. cit.,* note 168.
4. *Church History* 3:19.
5. Acts 9:2.
6. I Macc. 15:16-21.
7. Acts 18:12.
8. See V. M. Scramuzza, The Policy of the Early Roman Emperors toward Judaism (*The Beginnings of Christianity,* Vol. V, pp. 277-297).
9. Acts 18:14-15.
10. *Ibid.,* 21:26-28.
11. Chapter V, present volume.
12. Acts 21:38; for further discussion of the *Sicarii* see Chapter III of the present volume. The text of the King James Version of the Bible reads: "murderers." However, the Greek text has *Sicarii.* The word *Sicarii* Josephus applied to a particular party whose last leader was Eleazar, son of Jairus, a descendant of Judas of Galilee, to differentiate them from the parties led by John of Gishcala, Simon, the son of Gioras, and from the Zealots lead by Eleazar, the son of Simon. The word *Sicarii* was taken over by Josephus from the Latin *Sicarius.* It was never used in the Greek literature before Josephus. To make it clear to the Greek readers, Josephus had to explain why they were called *Sicarii.* He said because they "carried a little sword (a dagger) in their bosom." *Jewish War* 2:17,6.
13. Acts 23:6.

14. *Talmud Kiddushim* 43a.
15. Acts 23:9.
16. *Ibid.*
17. *Ibid.,* 23:26-30.
18. Compare I Macc. 15:21.
19. Acts 24:1-6.
20. *Ibid.,* 24:21.
21. *Ibid.,* 25:1-3.
22. Thomas of Harkel, bishop of Mabog, lived at the end of the sixth century.
23. Acts 25:5.
24. *Ibid.,* 8.
25. *Ibid.,* 19.
26. *Ibid.,* 9.
27. *Ibid.,* 10.
28. *Ibid.,* 26:32.
29. *Church History* 3:1.
30. *De praescriptione Haer.* chap. 36.
31. *Op. cit.,* 2,25.
32. *Histories* 5,9.
33. *Annals* 12,54.
34. See M. S. Enslin, *Christian Beginnings,* p. 422; see also H. Cadbury *The Making of Luke—Acts.*
35. See Goguel, *The Life of Jesus.*
36. Acts 21:11.

SELECTIVE BIBLIOGRAPHY

JEWISH HISTORY

MOORE, G. F. *Judaism in the First Centuries of the Christian Era, The Age of the Tannaim.*

HERFORD, T. *The Pharisees.*[1]

JACKSON, FOAKES and LAKE, KIRSOPP (editors). The Beginnings of Christianity, Vol. I;[2] Vol. V.[3]

FELTEN, J. *Neutestamentliche Zeitgeschichte oder Judentum und Heidentum zur Zeit Christi und der Apostel.*[4]

LAGRANGE, M. J. *Le Judaisme avant Jesus-Christ.*[5]

MATHEWS, S. *New Testament Times in Palestine.*

GUIGNEBERT, CH. *The Jewish World in the Time of Jesus.*[6]

OSTERLEY, W. O. E. *Judaism and Christianity,* Vol. I.[7]

ENSLIN, M. S. *Christian Beginnings,* Part 1.

ALBRIGHT, W. F. *From the Stone Age to Christianity,* chap. 6.

GOSPELS

ALLEN, W. C. *A Critical and Exegetical Commentary on the Gospel according to St. Matthew.*

GOULD, E. P. *A Critical and Exegetical Commentary on the Gospel according to St. Mark.*

PLUMMER, A. *A Critical and Exegetical Commentary on the Gospel according to St. Luke.*

TORREY, C. C. *Our Translated Gospels; Documents of the Primitive Church.*[8]

EASTON. *The Gospel before the Gospels.*

[1] *Jewish Quarterly Review* No. 16, 1926.
[2] *Ibid.* No. 14, 1923.
[3] *Ibid.* No. 25, 1934.
[4] *Ibid.* No. 25, 1934.
[5] *Ibid.* No. 25, 1934.
[6] *Ibid.* No. 30, 1940.
[7] *Ibid.* No. 29, 1934.
[8] *Ibid.* No. 32, 1942.

Stanton, V. H. *The Gospels as Historical Documents.*
Cadbury, H. J. *The Making of Luke—Acts.*
Lake, Kirsopp, and Cadbury, Henry. *The Acts of the Apostles.*
Zahn, Th. *Introduction to the New Testament.*
Dalman. *Jesus-Jeschua, Studies in the Gospels.*
Grant, F. C. *The Growth of the Gospels.*
Scott, E. F. *The Literature of the New Testament.*
Goodspeed, E. J. *An Introduction to the New Testament.*
Enslin, Morton Scott. *Christian Beginnings.*

THE LIFE OF JESUS

Klausner, J. *Jesus of Nazareth, His Life, Times and Teachings.*[9]
Barton, G. A. *Jesus of Nazareth, a Biography.*
Case, S. J. *Jesus, a New Biography.*
MacKinnon, J. *The Historic Jesus.*
Burkitt, F. C. *Jesus Christ, an Historical Outline.*
Goguel, M. *The Life of Jesus.*[10]
Olmstead, A. T. *Jesus in the Light of History.*

THE TRIAL OF JESUS

Husband, R. W. *The Prosecution of Jesus, Its Date, History and Legality.*
Radin, M. *The Trial of Jesus of Nazareth.*

All the works dealing with the life of Jesus deal with the trial as well.

[9] *Ibid.* No. 14, 1923.
[10] *Ibid.* No. 27, 1937.

Hoenig, S. B. *The Great Sanhedrin,* 1953.
Enslin, M. S. *The Prophet from Nazareth,* 1961.

APPENDIX

THE SYNEDRION AND THE SANHEDRIN

It is well known that the word "Sanhedrin" is of Greek origin—*synedrion*. *Synedrion* has the meaning of any kind of assembly or gathering of people. From the Greek literature it appears that the *synedrion* was not a permanent institution, but was invoked by the rulers of the state for advice and consultation whenever the need arose.

I

The term is used by Herodotus (484-425 B.C.E.) in numerous places in the sense of an assembly convened for a certain purpose. At the time of the capture and burning of the hall of the Acropolis, the Greeks of Salamis were divided in their opinion as to the continuation of the war. Those who were for the continuation of the struggle, Herodotus relates, left the conference (*synedrion*) and embarked on their vessels to fight on further. In another passage he narrates that, when Themistocles on one occasion found the Peloponnesians were outvoting him, he left the meeting (*synedrion*). Herodotus further states that Aegina Aristides, an Athenian, once came to the place of the council (*synedrion*), and called Themistocles out.

Xenophon (434-355 B.C.E.) and various other Greek authors also used the word *synedrion*. In his *Hellenica*, Xenophon says that Hermocrates enjoyed the greatest reputation in the general council (*synedrion*). In his *Memorabilia* he states that Euthydemus was reluctant to join the council (*synedrias*).

Isocrates (436-388 B.C.E.) in his oration to Nicocles, in contrasting the inefficiency of a democracy as against the advantage of a monarchy, declared: "When they assemble in *synedria* you will find them more often quarreling with each other than deliberating together, while the latter (the monarchy) for whom no *synedrion* or times of meetings are prescribed, but who apply themselves to the state's business both day and night, do not let opportunities pass them but act in each case at the right moment."

The historians Thucydides (460-395 B.C.E.) and Polybius also used *synedrion* in the sense of an assembly. Polybius (205-125 B.C.E.) states that during the wars in which the Romans were engaged against Hannibal, Tiberius (the consul) had many conferences (*synedreue*) with Publius Scipio. In another passage Polybius used *synedrion* with the meaning of a meeting or conference. He says that "the leaders of the Gauls, on seeing the camp-fires at night, surmised that the enemy had arrived, and held a council (*synedrion*)."

Similarly, the term *synedrion* was used by the noted Greek orator Lysias (450-380 B.C.E.). (*For the Soldier, 9-11.*) Aeschinus (389-314) used the term *synedrion* in the sense of a meeting place—assembly house. In his speech against Ctesophon he said, "You could have made that former peace, fellow Athenians, supported by the joint action of the conference (*synedriou*) of the Greek states." In the same manner *synedrion* was used by Demosthenes (384-322). That Lysias and Demosthenes used *synedrion* in the sense of assembly and not "court" is evident from their orations before the court, for in addressing the court they always used the phrase "fellow judges" (*andres dikastoi*) but never *andres synedroi*. As a matter of fact, *synedroi* was never used in the entire Greek literature in the sense of members of the court, because *synedrion* did not have the connotation of a court but of a council. Thus, the term *synedrioi* could not be used. The first time the term *andres synedroi* was used was in the book, *Antiquities*, written by Josephus *circa* 93 C.E.

Strabo the geographer and historian, who was a contemporary of Jesus and who died shortly before the crucifixion, also used *synedrion* in the sense of a conference. Of the members of the Lycian League who had the right to vote, he says: "They came together from each city to a general conference *synedrion*. . . . At the conference (*synedrio*) they first choose a Lyciarch and then other officials of the league, and the courts of justice are designated."

Synedrion occurs frequently in Judeo-Hellenistic literature in the sense of assembly or council.

The author of II Maccabees tells us that when Demetrius ascended the throne, Alcimus went to see him and complained about Judas Maccabeus. Demetrius called Alcimus. into a conference (*synedrion*). It is well known that II Maccabees is an epitome of a larger work by Jason of Cyrene. This book was written in Greek and made use of Greek sources. Thus we see that *synedrion* was used in Greek literature in the sense of conference or council. either military or civil.

The Septuagint version of the Pentateuch never uses *synedrion*. In the Septuagint version of Jeremiah *synedrion* occurs only once. Likewise, in the Book of Psalms *synedrion* is also found only once. In the Book of Proverbs *synedrion* occurs eight times in the sense of council. The exact date of the Greek translation of these biblical books, however, cannot be ascertained.

In the Book of Ben Sirah *synedros* has the meaning of "to sit together," as in chapter 11:9: "Sit not (*synedreue*) in judgment with sinners." In chapter 23:14 we find: "Remember your father and your mother when thou sittest (*synedreuis*) among great men." In chapter 42:12 we read: "And sit (*synedreus*) not in the midst of a woman." In the Book of Judith *synedria* was used in the sense of a council, e.g., the council of Holofernes.

In the Psalms of Solomon, which has come down to us in Greek, but the original of which was in Hebrew, we have *synedrion* again used in the sense of a council; similarly in IV Maccabees.

Philo in his writings mentions *synedros* and *synedrion* quite frequently in the sense of councilor and assembly or council. He also refers metaphorically to the soul as the assembly (*synedrion*) of the body.

Josephus, likewise, used *synedrion* quite often in his works. In his book *Jewish War, synedrion* is always used in the sense of council or conference. Josephus tells us that when Herod presented his case against his sons to Augustus Caesar, Augustus granted him complete liberty of action, advising Herod "to hold an inquiry into their plot before a joint council (*synedrion*) of his own relatives and provincial governors." In another passage Josephus says that when Herod became indignant at the wife of his brother, Pheroras, he "assembled a council (*synedrion*) of his friends and relatives, and accused this wretched woman of numerous misdeeds." Josephus further relates that when Herod became aware of the plots of his son, Antipater, on arriving at Jerusalem, he "assembled a council (*synedrion*) of his relatives and friends, inviting Antipater's friends to attend as well." In another passage the historian says that after the death of Herod, when the rivals for the kingdom of Judea presented their cases for Augustus to decide, the emperor "summoned a council (*synedrion*) of the leading Romans." He invited the rivals to state their cases before his council (*synedrous*). Josephus further relates that "after dismissing his council (*synedrous*), he [Augustus] passed the day in reflection on what he had heard." Josephus again records that when a Jewish embassy came to Rome to present their case, "Caesar assembled a council (*synedrion*) composed of the Roman magistrates and his friends in the temple of Palatine Apollo." After hearing the case presented by the embassy he "dismissed the council (*synedrion*)."

In Josephus' *Antiquities of the Jews, synedrion* appears many times. Josephus tells us that Gabanius divided the country of Judea into five councils (*synedria*). He relates that when Herod was accused of killing innocent men while he was governor of Galilee, he was summoned to appear before a *synedrion*. Here for *the first and only time* Josephus uses the term *synedrion* in the sense of a court. In all other cases he does not use *synedrion* in the sense of a court but of a council or assembly, called by the ruler for a particular purpose. He tells us that Herod, in order to find a reason for executing the deposed king Hyrkanus, produced a letter before the *synedrion* which Hyrkanus had written to Malchus. Josephus further relates that when the Levites insisted that King Agrippa allow them to wear linen garments such as were worn by the priests, Agrippa called a *synedrion* which gave them permission to do so. Josephus further states that the high priest appointed a *synedrion* (council) of judges and charged James (the brother of Jesus) with transgression.

Josephus in his *Vita* says that after his arrival in Galilee, he wrote a full report to the *synedrion* (council) of Jerusalem about conditions in the country. This council was organized after the Jews were victorious over the Roman general Cestius. Josephus also states that when he settled the affairs in Tiberias, he assembled his friends in a council (*synedrion*). Thus we see that *synedrion* in the sense of a court was used as such for the first time by Josephus in his *Antiquities of the Jews*, published in the year 93 C.E.

II

There is no doubt that in the early period of Jewish history there was no organized court as such. In Exodus we read: "But if a servant shall plainly say, 'I love my master, my wife, my children, I will not go out free'; then his master shall bring him unto *Elohim*." The rabbis interpreted the word *Elohim* to mean "judges." The Septuagint also renders this word "the court of God." In the same book it is further written: "For every matter of trespass, whether it be for an ox . . . both parties shall come before *Elohim*; he whom *Elohim* shall condemn shall pay double unto his neighbour." Exodus also tells us that Moses judged the people, but that his father-in-law, Jethro, advised him to appoint men who should help him in this task. Only a matter of great importance, he told Moses, should be brought before him, while small matters should be judged by the appointees. In Deuteronomy we read that the Jews were directed to appoint judges and officers in the cities who were to judge the people with righteous judgment. In the same book we are told: "If there arise a matter too hard for thee in judgment. . . . And thou shalt come unto the priests, the Levites, and unto the judge that shall be in those days; and thou shalt inquire; and they shall declare unto thee the sentence of judgment."

Was there thus instituted a court of justice in the early days of Jewish history? There is no historical evidence of such an institution. According to the Bible, Moses was the chief justice, and on his death Joshua became the supreme judge. After the death of Joshua, those who saved the Jews from their oppressors by military exploits became judges. In Judges it says: "When God raised them up judges, then God was with the judge, and saved them out of the hands of their enemies all the days of the judge." Othniel, the son of Kenaz, judged Israel because he had defeated the king of Aram. In fact, all the men who helped the Israelites defeat their enemies became their leaders and judges. Among them was a woman named Deborah, who also judged the children of Israel; she had participated in the defeat of Sisera, the captain of the king of Canaan. The prophet Samuel was also a chief judge of Israel. When he became old he appointed his sons judges of Israel. However, his sons were not righteous and took bribes and perverted justice. Then, according to the Bible, the elders assembled and came to Samuel, and said to him, "Behold, thou art old and thy sons walk not in thy ways; now make us a king to judge us like all the nations."

The duty of the king was not only to rule the people and defend them against their enemies in war, but also to act as judge in their personal quarrels. The author of II Samuel relates that when Absalom plotted for the throne of his father David, he used to rise early to meet the men who "had a suit which should come to the king for judgment," and that he used to tell the people: "Oh that I were made judge in the land, that every man who hath any suit or cause might come unto me, and I would do him justice." Solomon, after ascending the throne of his father, prayed to God that among other things God should grant him "an understanding heart to judge." Indeed, to show that God had granted him "a heart to judge," the Bible relates the well-known story of the quarrel between the two women who were harlots, as to who was the mother of the child each claimed.

Thus, we may surmise that the kings were themselves judges and that they appointed judges in different cities who were subordinate to themselves. According to Aristotle, it was the custom in all the states where lawful monarchy ruled that the kings were judges. Aristotle tells us that they had supreme command in war and they controlled all the sacrifices that were not in the hands of the priestly class. In addition to these functions, they were judges. Some gave judgment on oath (the oath was taken by holding up the scepter), and some did not.

III

With the Restoration supreme authority over the Jews was vested in the high priests. This authority was conferred upon the high priests by the subsequent kings of Persia, and later by the Ptolemian and Seleucidean rulers. The Pentateuch was canonized at that time. According to Deuteronomy, the right to judge and instruct the Jews was given to the priests. Since jurisdiction over the Jews was vested in the high priest-pontiff who had sole authority over the Jewish people, the new Jewish settlement was established as a theocracy. Hence the authority to judge the Jews was transferred from the kings to the priests.

In the decree which the Persian king gave to Ezra authorizing him to appoint judges, the term *dayyan* was used. *Dayyan* became the accepted term for a judge, and the term for court was *Bet Din*. The head of the court was designated

Ab-Bet-Din. It is more than likely that the high priests during the period of the theocracy had the title *Nasi.* That the court was called *Bet Din* is quite evident from the early Tannaitic literature, but it is also obvious from the early Judeo-Hellenistic literature. For example, the author of the Book of Susannah tells us that two elders accused Susannah of adultery, and that she was condemned to death. However, a young man named Daniel protested against the verdict and told the people that these elders had testified falsely. She was brought back to the *Bet Din,* courthouse. The men who tried her were called *dayyanim,* judges.

With the transformation from a theocracy to a Commonwealth a fundamental change in the judicial system resulted. In the pre-Maccabean period the high priest, being the pontifical head of all the Jews, had the sole authority to instruct the people and to interpret the religious laws. However, after the establishment of the Commonwealth, the high priest was shorn of all his authority as the head of all the Jews. He no longer had the right to appoint religious judges. Neither did the civil ruler have the right to interpret religious laws. As ethnarch or king his authority was only political and civil, not religious, and his domain was only Judea. The change from theocracy to Commonwealth had a profound influence upon the whole of Jewish life and it had to undergo a thorough readjustment. The judiciary system, likewise, went through a radical transformation.

IV

With the establishment of the Commonwealth a court was instituted independent of the high priest and the ethnarch, to try religious offenders. It consisted of twenty-three members and it had a seat in every important town. There were three such courts in Jerusalem, including the Temple area. These courts were only trial courts and had no right to legislate. During the period of the theocracy the high priest was the supreme authority and he interpreted the religious laws; but now that he was shorn of this authority, a new institution was established as a legislative body. It was known as *Bet Din HaGadol*, the Great Court, and consisted of seventy-one members. Thus, the judiciary system in Judea consisted of two branches, the trial court and the legislative court. The Great Court made the laws by interpreting the Pentateuch.

The lower courts and the Great Court decided cases of offenders against the religious laws. The Great Court passed laws which affected the lives not only of the Jews in Judea but of the Jews throughout the world. The ordinary court of twenty-three tried religious cases, those that the Persian king in his edict to Ezra called "the laws of God." However, cases affecting the state or the ruler himself were beyond the jurisdiction of this court. The only authority over such matters was held by the ruler, the king. When Herod sought to destroy his enemies, whom he suspected of plotting against his sovereignty, he summoned a council of his own men and friends who constituted a court and it was called by the Greek name *synedrion.*

V

After the destruction of the Second Temple in the year 70 C.E. the Jews were deprived of their political independence. With the burning of the Temple, the position of the high priest was gone. The only remaining authority was the religious court, which had jurisdiction over the whole of Jewry. In Judea, however, the religious court assumed the supervision of Jewish life and represented the Jews of Judea before the Roman authorities. This responsibility that was formerly held by the high priests was transferred to the religious court. The religious court, which before the destruction of the Temple had no civil authority or responsibility, dealt also with civil matters after the destruction. Thus, *synedrion*, which before the destruction of the Temple had been used in connection with the councils that were summoned first by the kings and later by the high priests for political and civil matters, was now used to designate the religious court, since it also took up civil matters. Therefore, after the destruction of the Temple the court was called by its old name, *Bet Din*, and also by the Hebraic term for the Greek *synedrion*, Sanhedrin. The name "Sanhedrin," as applied to the religious court of Judea, was even Latinized. Theodosius, in his laws against the Jews, used the phrase *Palaestinae Synedriis*.

The term "Sanhedrin," as a matter of fact, never occurs prior to the destruction of the Temple in Tannaitic literature. Only in the Tannaitic literature of the period after the destruction of the Temple does the name "Sanhedrin" occur. Although Sanhedrin became synonomous with *Bet Din*, the old term *Ab-Bet-Din* for the head of the court remained. The individual member of the court was still calley *dayyan*. The Talmud never uses a singular form of the collective term "Sanhedrin." As we have remarked in the previous passages, the term "Sanhedrin" never occurs in the Septuagint version of the Pentateuch. In the entire Judeo-Hellenistic literature the term *synedrion* in the sense of the Jewish court does not occur.

It might further be pointed out that significantly the Vulgate renders *synedrion* in the Gospels by *concilium*, and not by *judicium*, which we would expect if this *synedrion* was a court. From this we may surmise that even the authors of the Vulgate knew that Jesus was tried by a *concilium*, an assembly, a state *synedrion*, and not by a Jewish court, or Sanhedrin (*Bet Din*).

GENERAL INDEX

Aaron, 9
Ab Bet Din, 70, 139
Abner, 118
Acts, vii
  source for the trials of Peter, Paul, and Stephen, 181-186
  when and for whom written, 205-206
Adultery, 123-124
Agriculture
  in Galilee, 66
  in the Persian period, 15
Agrippa I, 55-56, 80, 82, 188, 203, 204, 224
Agrippa II, King of Chalcis, 56, 57, 82-83
Akiba, 123
Albinus, 59, 82, 83, 158
Albright, W. F., 218
Alexander of Macedonia, 13-14
Alexander (son of Aristobulus), 40
Alexander (son of Herod), 46, 79
Alexandra
  execution of, 46
  reign of, 37
Allen, W., 219
Ame Ha-aretz, see Farmers
Ananias, 201
Ananus, 82, 83
Anger, 125-127
Annas, 148
Annius Rufus, 52
Anthony, 41, 42
Antigonus, 41
"Antiochenes," 16, 17
Antiochus Epiphanes, 16-17, 22
Antipater, machinations of, 37-38, 40
Antipater (son of Herod), 46

Apocalyptic-Pharisees, 91, 96-100, 157, 158, 168, 209
  beliefs of, 99
Apostolic Fathers, vii, 3, 4, 179
Appeasement
  religious, xiii
  of Rome by Christians, 174-177, 206-207
"Appeasers," high priests as, 156, 157
Archelaus, 49
Aristobulus (son of Alexandra)
  death of, 42-43, 45
  wars of, with Hyrcanus, 37-39, 40, 44
Aristobulus (son of Herod), 46, 79
Aristobulus (son of John Hyrcanus), 36
Aristocracy, 35-36
  murder of, 42, 43
Arrest of Jesus, discrepancies in account of, 150-151
Artaxerxes, 8
Asahel, 118
Assimilation, 16-17, 35
  revolt against, 18-23
Augustus Caesar, 40, 42, 49, 55, 74, 91
"Avenger of the Blood," 117, 118

Baal-Shem-Tob, Rabbi Israel, 136-137
Babylon, Jews in, 8
Barabbas, 149, 166-167
Bathsheba, 107
Beginnings of Christianity, The, vii
Ben Sirah, 20, 213, 220
Bevan, 213

239

INDEX OF WORKS CITED